PLAN YOUR

# WARDROBE

WITH

## *Chata Romano*

# PLAN YOUR
# WARDROBE
## WITH
# *Chata Romano*

First published in 1998 by
New Holland Publishers (UK) Ltd
London • Cape Town • Sydney • Auckland

Copyright in text © Chata Romano (Pty) Ltd 1998
Copyright in photographs © New Holland Publishers (UK) Ltd 1998,
except the following: Revlon, Inc.: pp. 4 (top right), 128, 129, 131;
Stuttafords: pp. 55, 58, 59, 68, 74, 77, 81, 83, 89, 104; American Swiss: p. 63
Copyright in illustrations © New Holland Publishers (UK) Ltd 1998,
except the following: Revlon, Inc.: pp. 132–145
Copyright in published edition © New Holland Publishers (UK) Ltd 1998

ISBN 1 85974 940 2 (pb)

**Editor:** Joy Clack
**Designer:** Petal Palmer
**Assistant designer:** Lellyn Creamer
**Photographers:** Ian Reeves, Jillian Lochner and David Ross
**Illustrator:** Maryna Bergh
**Hair & make-up:** Hannon Bothma, Karl Isaacs, Dulcie Beebe and Lynne Hacker
**Locations:** Peninsula Hotel, Mount Nelson and the home of Paula Davies

Reproduction by Hirt & Carter Cape (Pty) Ltd
Printed and bound in Singapore by Tien Wah Press (Pte) Ltd

2 4 6 8 10 9 7 5 3

# ACKNOWLEDGEMENTS

To Avri, my husband. To think that it all began on the day you sold your house to start our business – you did not know what would happen yet you had absolute faith in me. Thank you for your unwavering love and your tremendous ability to manage and run our business with such skill. But mostly, thank you for your gorgeous smile that constantly lights up my life. Always '*Kol ma sheanagnoo, nagon!*'

I would also like to thank all my clients for their letters of enthusiasm, encouragement and good wishes. I appreciate every one.

To the dream team from Struik – Joy, Petal, Linda and Lois – thank you for sharing the same vision as us, for your unwavering support, friendly smiles and expertise.

And to the team with which I have worked so closely – photographers, hairdressers, make-up artists and assistants – I could not have done it without you. Your work is pure genius, your talents so vast, and your humour unique. Thank you.

It has been incredibly rewarding to see our makeover ladies leaving us at the end of the day looking and feeling their best, and to see how their lives have changed accordingly. Thank you for letting me wave my magic wand.

Thank you to *Essentials, Rooi Rose, Sarie* and *Longevity* magazines for their continuing support.

A very special word of thanks to our sponsors, Revlon, Stuttafords, American Swiss and Clairol.

And last, but certainly not least, Philip Smith. Thank you for believing in us right from the very beginning.

# CONTENTS

## AUTHOR'S NOTE

I WOULD LIKE to thank all my clients who have come to see me over the past few years, looking for direction and trying to make the best of a very confusing fashion world. Through your continuing support you have inspired me to go forward and do what I love doing best – helping people. The satisfaction and gratitude I feel has always been the driving force behind me, and is what has inspired me to write this book.

I have received so many wonderful letters over the years and I thank you for all of them – they have really touched my heart, especially those of you who at first felt despondent, desperate and believed there was no hope.

One of my clients felt somewhat intimidated about coming to see me but on the strong recommendation of her friend she did. At the end of the appointment she turned around and said to me:

'Chata, when I booked the appointment, I was very nervous. I heard about you from various friends, read all your articles and saw your makeovers. Although you have consistently used ordinary people and not models, they always looked so slim and beautiful. And there I was, feeling unhappy and overweight. I really thought there was no hope for me.

'Since my appointment with you I feel like a completely different person! I now look elegant and fashionable – you have given me an individual look which is right for me. I feel fantastic when I look in the mirror and see a slimmer me. At the end of my appointment with you, I felt so beautiful!'

I look forward to sharing this new beginning with you in anticipation that the joy you feel in learning how to express your individuality in the way you dress will grow from day to day.

The aim is to see that special gleam of appreciation in the eyes of those whose opinions matter most to you – but above all to see it in your own eyes.

# INTRODUCTION

A GOOD COLLECTION of clothing is an investment in self-esteem, a vital part of one's strategy for self-fulfilment.

I would like to give you a few statistics about myself as, against all assumptions, I'm not one of those super tall, super slim fashion models. I am 33 years old, 1.52 m (5 ft 2 in) and weigh 50 kg (110 lb).

Much of my work is based on my knees, having spent my life trying to disguise a really bad pair. In my workshops I bravely raise the hemline of my knee-length skirt by just 3 cm (1¼ in) (which isn't all that much) and invite comments from the audience, over whom an embarrassed hush usually falls. 'Come on,' I encourage, 'say what you like, be honest. How do I look now? I've heard it all before, so I promise not to be offended.'

'Fat', 'Frumpy', 'Shapeless', volunteer the frank and heartless. I am pleased. I then show them how to 'repair' the image by sliding my skirt 3 cm (1¼ in) down to mid-knee. 'What has happened now?' I ask them. 'Amazing, you look so tall and slim.' Needless to say, I am even more pleased. In a few seconds, the audience drastically changed their opinion of how I look. My body had not changed, I hadn't lost or gained weight – it was simply the correct length of my skirt that created such a different response.

Welcome to reality – nobody has a perfect figure! The question is, 'What do we do about it?' Instead of focusing on the faults, let's concentrate on highlighting the assets.

Realize the potential of your appearance and enjoy a renewed self-confidence. Incorrect appearance is not always due to the shortcomings of your body, but rather due to the clothes that you wear.

When you wake up in the morning, what is the very first thought that crosses your mind? Is it 'What am I going to wear today?' or 'I have nothing to wear!'?

Because you have three wardrobes filled with clothes it does not mean you have something to wear. On the contrary, you are most probably more confused. Do not despair, you are not alone with these agonizing dilemmas – most of the world experiences the same frustrations. Let our goal be to eliminate them once and for all.

This book has been written in the most practical way possible. I trust that it will show you, both visually and practically, how to make your wardrobe work for you. Wardrobe planning is fascinating and vital to success. It is about self-knowledge and attainable aspirations, investment and return, perception and proportion, creative expression and skill.

The learning curve is discovering what makes you look your best. Investment dressing has never been more important. There is no better way to succeed over the competition than to be noticed and remembered through clothes. By being in the right state of mind when you shop, you'll avoid those impulse buys that ultimately prove to be a waste.

Research says that an impression is created within 45 seconds of meeting a person for the first time – I say the first second.

Every wardrobe, whatever spending power it represents, contains its fair share of misfits, disappointments and downright disasters. As budgets shrink and fashion messages conflict in our fast-changing markets, it becomes more and more difficult to know what to buy, how much to spend, how to distinguish between good quality fashion basics, genuine trends and passing fads, how much to invest in lasting quality and what to buy for fun. More importantly, it becomes more difficult to know what to wear and how to wear it.

Planning our life at home and at work comes to us naturally, but when it comes to planning our wardrobes we are left out in the cold without guidance. There is no way of knowing how to interpret and understand fashion other than from fashion magazines. That is why we often come up short financially when buying fashion incorrectly.

Take the doubt out of dressing by learning style strategies.

There are two things that make you different. How you see the world and how the world sees you.

Only once you're sure of the path you're on, can you dress for the journey. If you follow the guidelines in this book, you will never again have to ask that frustrating question 'What am I going to wear today?'

# CHAPTER ONE

# COLOUR

*'True beauty is simplicity'*
ISSEY MIYAKE

YOU GET DRESSED in the morning, look in the mirror, and like what you see. The comments you receive during the day are 'You look fantastic!', 'That colour looks amazing on you', and, your all time favourite, 'Have you lost weight?' At the end of the day you feel motivated and confident.

That night you go to bed early and sleep like a baby. The next morning you wake feeling refreshed, energetic and you are in a very good mood. You get dressed, look in the mirror and don't really like the outfit you are wearing but you shrug it off because you feel really good inside. The very first person that you see at 8.00 am asks: 'Did you have a late night?', 'Are you feeling ill?' Compared with the positive comments you received the previous day, these definitely aren't the same and by the end of the day you feel depressed and demotivated.

You should only be hearing positive comments, whether you are smartly dressed for a special occasion or casually in jeans and a shirt. Perhaps it is unfair, but most people judge you not by how you feel inside but by how you project yourself, and the first thing they notice (from a distance) is the colour you are wearing. Colour makes a huge difference to the way you project yourself and the way others react to you. Although it is important to always look and feel your best, colour is only one piece of the puzzle and is no more important than style, fabric and proportions.

Few people can wear pale, muted or dirty colours next to their face. You may have a beautiful, healthy skin but wearing pale colours will make you look tired. Stand in front of your mirror in good daylight and hold any pale colour next to your face. Look at your eyes and skin tone. Do you not look tired and drained? Do you want to add additional blusher or lipstick?

Mid-tone, clean and bright colours will give your face life, colour and a

*Chata demonstrating the correct and incorrect colours for this skin tone. The correct colour is the one on the right.*

*The blue over the left shoulder is too pale for this skin tone, whereas the blue on the right shoulder is clean and clear.*

natural sparkle. The colours that you wear must look perfect next to your face without any make-up or accessories. The correct colours should enhance what already looks good.

The most important aspect to remember about colour is that you cannot always wear the colours that you like. You must only wear the colours that are the best for you and from these choose the ones you like. Simply leave out the colours that you don't like or don't feel happy wearing. There may be certain colours you love but which do not appear on your colour chart. They are not there because they do not love you!

In the fashion world, designers select a specific colour range for the summer, autumn, winter and spring seasons. The manufacturers then produce the merchandise and send it to the stores. There may be some colours that suit you and some that do not, but within each season there will always be colours that are right for you. It is interesting that most people can wear most colours, but it's the

intensity and level of the colour's shade that make it right or wrong. Take red for example – you may look great wearing a deep, rich red but not an orange-red. They are both red, but the intensity and tone differs.

Your wardrobe should consist of approximately 60% colour and 40% basic. You cannot leave out the basics (navy, black, white, stone, brown, grey) because colours (blues, greens, pinks, etc.) will not co-ordinate without them. However, if you have only the basics, you will end up looking the same every day and will probably feel boring and dowdy.

If you are uncomfortable wearing bright colours, such as emerald green, don't buy a matching emerald green jacket and skirt. Rather wear the green jacket with a navy pencil skirt and reduce the colour to only 30%. Or try a navy suit with an emerald green silk blouse or camisole – you will have further reduced the colour to 10%.

There are many colour consultants who will analyze your colours for you, each with their own system. Some

suggest colours that range from the lightest to the darkest, others work according to the seasons, and some have the theory that your eye colour determines what you should wear. Some will even say: 'You have a very yellow tone to your skin and therefore you must wear yellow-based colours.' If you took their advice your skin tone would look even more yellow!

I have developed a new, easy-to-follow system to determine which colours you should wear.

If your wardrobe consists of a mixture of light, dark, medium, pale and bright colours, very little of what you have will ever co-ordinate. My system enables you to work with colours of the same level of intensity, ensuring continuity and making it easy to mix and match different garments. From now on, each item you purchase will, without much effort on your part, co-ordinate with two, three or even four items in your existing wardrobe.

In the following pages you will discover the different colours that are best suited to your skin tone.

Please note that you cannot look at the skin tone on your hands to determine what colours are best for you as you don't wear colours on your hands, you wear them next to your face. The skin tone of your hand is also completely different from that of your face.

The colour of your hair is also an important factor to consider. Your colours will not change when you change the colour of your hair, providing the hair colour you choose suits your skin tone.

Before we continue, it is important that you understand my technique of colour analysis. I have listed three different levels of colours on the following page. Look at these and the 'colour personality' of each group.

1. DIRTY COLOURS: Lifeless, sludgy, murky, dull.

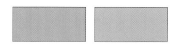

2. MEDIUM COLOURS: Rich, deep, lustrous.

3. CLEAR COLOURS: Light, clean, fresh, crisp.

Let's begin with what no one should do – wear dirty colours. The description of dirty colours is lifeless, sludgy, murky and dull. Why would you want to wear colours like this next to the most important part of your body – your face?

Below is a test to ensure that you clearly understand the difference between clean and dirty colours.

Which are the clean colours in the following list?

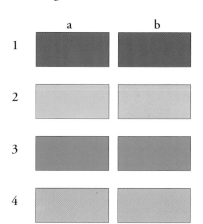

*Answers: 1b, 2a, 3a, 4b*

## BLACK

◆ Black works best with warm colours and looks reasonable with some cool colours (see colour definitions, page 96). For example, black won't work with turquoise as there is no warmth or connection between the two colours. However, put turquoise with navy and see how much richer and softer the colours look together. Navy will work with just about any of the hot or cold colours. French navy is so dark it is almost black, and co-ordinates well with all levels of colour.

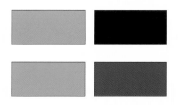

◆ Wearing black on the top half of the body does not suit everyone, but almost anyone can wear it at the bottom. Black is too hard to wear next to your face, especially if you have a fair skin. It makes you look tired, drained and unapproachable, especially as you get older. Rather wear black away from your face, either as a bottom or as a jacket with a lighter (or brighter) colour underneath it.

◆ The only people who can wear black as a polo neck are those with contrasting tones such as black hair and a pale white skin.

◆ Black can be dressed up and down. A simple black dress can be worn with sandals during the day or with stunning shoes for the evening.

◆ Black can be very slimming and can project many different images – elegant, dramatic, chic, sexy or even mournful. It is a colour that never dates and can be worn year after year, winter or summer.

# IDENTIFYING YOUR COLOURS

There are three levels of colour but you will only suit one group. You will either suit Soft, Medium or Deep colours. Look at the before and after photographs for each colour group and you will see how important it is to wear the correct colours.

**Before:** *Avoid wearing dark colours if you have fair skin.*

**After:** *Wearing clean, clear colours will make your skin sparkle.*

**Before:** *Avoid wearing grey on the top half of your body as it will add years to your age.*

**After:** *Strong, rich colours will create a look of energy and vitality.*

**Opposite:** *Pale colours (before) make you look tired, whereas deep, rich colours (after) add lustre.*

# SOFT COLOURS
## (CLEAN, CLEAR, LIGHT AND FRESH)

NATURAL HAIR COLOUR
Ash blonde, light blonde to honey or golden blonde, light brown or grey.

EYES
Blue, grey, light green or light brown.

SKIN
Clear, ivory skin tone with rosy cheeks and light beige undertone.

*Please note:* Do not wear brilliant white as it will make you looked tired. You can wear winter white (off-white) or ivory (the colour of pearls) but not cream as it is too yellow.

Stone and grey should only be worn in pants and skirts. If you wear these colours in a shirt you will look tired and drained.

JEWELLERY
Silver.
Light gold.
Avoid very yellow gold.

SHOES, BAGS, BELTS
Rust.
Brown.
Navy.
Black.

**Before:** *Bottle green is too dark and heavy for a fair skin tone.*

**After:** *A new woman – soft colours make her look ten years younger!*

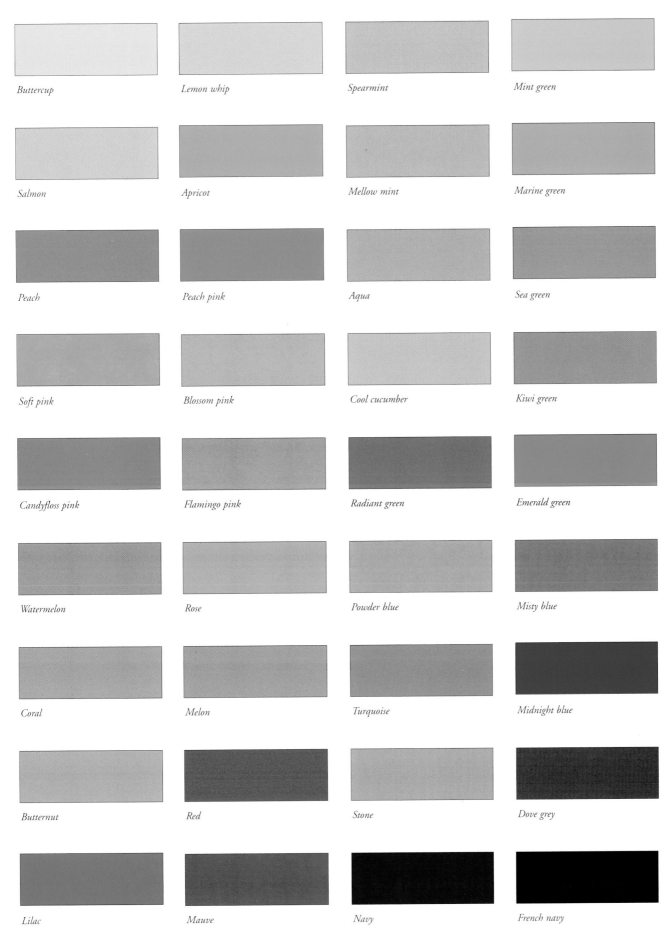

Buttercup

Lemon whip

Spearmint

Mint green

Salmon

Apricot

Mellow mint

Marine green

Peach

Peach pink

Aqua

Sea green

Soft pink

Blossom pink

Cool cucumber

Kiwi green

Candyfloss pink

Flamingo pink

Radiant green

Emerald green

Watermelon

Rose

Powder blue

Misty blue

Coral

Melon

Turquoise

Midnight blue

Butternut

Red

Stone

Dove grey

Lilac

Mauve

Navy

French navy

# MEDIUM COLOURS
## (CRISP, COOL, RICH, MEDIUM TO BRIGHT)

NATURAL HAIR COLOUR
Medium to dark brown or black.

EYES
Grey, green or dark brown.

SKIN
Delicate rosy tones or a natural tan. A pale skin contrasting with black or blue-black hair with shades of blueberry or blackberry.

*Please note:* White should only be worn in summer if you tan easily. You can also wear winter white (off-white) and ivory (the colour of pearls) but not cream as it is too yellow.

Stone can be worn in any style *except* as a high, round neck, such as a polo neck. You can wear it as a jacket with a winter-white blouse, camisole or body stocking underneath.

JEWELLERY
Silver or gold.
Silver will look better when you start going grey naturally.

SHOES, BAGS, BELTS
Brown.
Rust.
Tan.
Navy.
Black.

**Before:** *Dark colours worn too close to the face can make you look pale and drained.*

**After:** *A lower neckline in a dark colour can look elegant and sophisticated.*

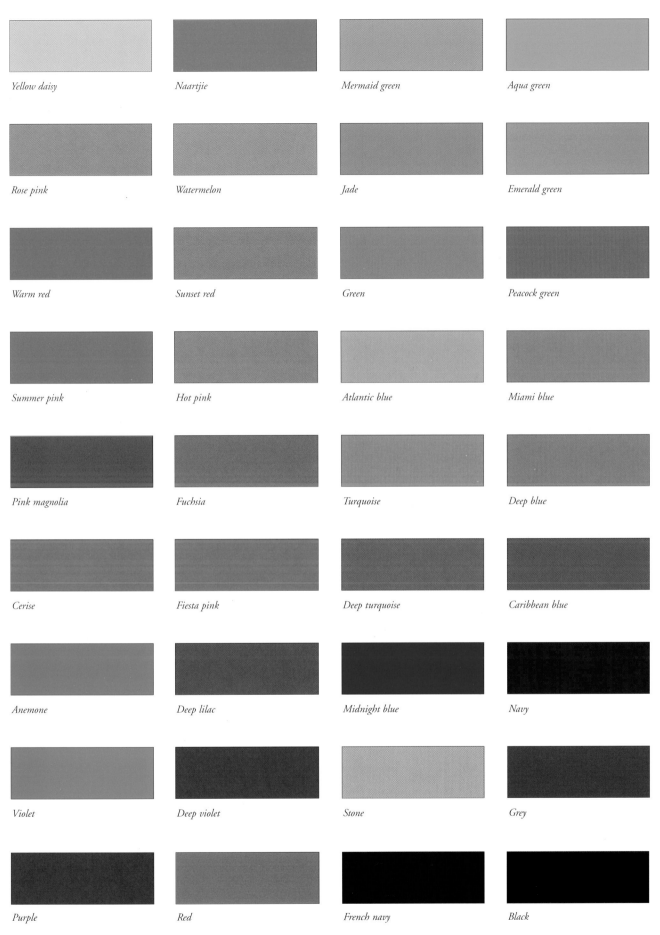

| | | | |
|---|---|---|---|
| Yellow daisy | Naartjie | Mermaid green | Aqua green |
| Rose pink | Watermelon | Jade | Emerald green |
| Warm red | Sunset red | Green | Peacock green |
| Summer pink | Hot pink | Atlantic blue | Miami blue |
| Pink magnolia | Fuchsia | Turquoise | Deep blue |
| Cerise | Fiesta pink | Deep turquoise | Caribbean blue |
| Anemone | Deep lilac | Midnight blue | Navy |
| Violet | Deep violet | Stone | Grey |
| Purple | Red | French navy | Black |

# DEEP COLOURS
## (LUSTROUS, DEEP, EARTHY, WITH WARM GOLDEN TONES)

**NATURAL HAIR COLOUR**
Red tones such as Titian red, copper, chestnut or hazelnut. Black with warm red tones such as mahogany and auburn, or rich black.

**EYES**
Bright blue, clear green, amber, hazel or black.

**SKIN**
Natural golden tan, often with freckles, or olive skin. Darker skin: Indian, Hispanic or Black.

*Please note:* You can wear white, winter white (off-white) or ivory (pearl colour), but not cream as it is too yellow.

Stone should never be worn as a high, round neck, such as a polo neck, as this will make you look tired. Rather wear it away from your face in a camisole, body stocking, jacket or as a skirt or pants.

**JEWELLERY**
Gold.

**SHOES, BAGS, BELTS**
Rust.
Tan.
Brown.
Navy or black.

**Before:** *Soft green is too pale and washed out for a deep skin tone.*

**After:** *Stronger, deeper emerald green adds light, life and lustre.*

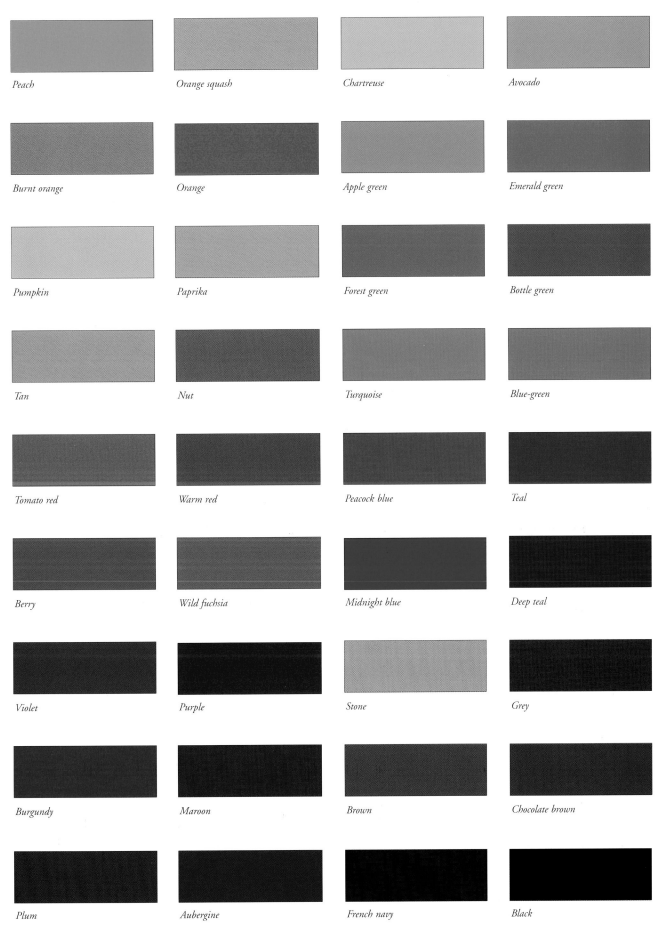

Peach

Orange squash

Chartreuse

Avocado

Burnt orange

Orange

Apple green

Emerald green

Pumpkin

Paprika

Forest green

Bottle green

Tan

Nut

Turquoise

Blue-green

Tomato red

Warm red

Peacock blue

Teal

Berry

Wild fuchsia

Midnight blue

Deep teal

Violet

Purple

Stone

Grey

Burgundy

Maroon

Brown

Chocolate brown

Plum

Aubergine

French navy

Black

# CHAPTER TWO

# STYLE

*'Fashions fade, style lingers'*
YVES ST LAURENT

DO YOU WANT to look taller and slimmer? Are you short- or long-waisted? Which skirt lengths work best for you – short or long? Do you have narrow, wide or balanced shoulders? Don't despair if you do not know the answers to these questions. This chapter will answer all of them.

So many of us gaze into the mirror and wish we looked like someone else. It is quite simple – you have two choices. You can be depressed for the rest of your life, or you can do something about it.

You don't need a magic wand or the sharp blade of a surgeon's scalpel to achieve a perfect body; all you need to

do is understand which lengths and styles work for you. You need to look at yourself in the mirror and forget about what is underneath your outfit. If your faults are concealed the right way, who's to know? More importantly, you won't be so self-conscious about it anymore.

Remember, without your clothes there is not much you can do about camouflaging figure faults, but if you wear the correct styles you will be amazed at what you can accomplish.

In this section I cover all the correct lengths, balances and proportions. These are vital to achieve a correct total look. A skirt can be either 4 cm

(1½ in) too long or too short and your proportion will be completely out of balance. Do you have a full-length mirror? If not, invest in one, as you must be able to see yourself from head to toe to establish your proportions and to fully appreciate the difference you will see.

You may have heard of the figure analysis system where your body shape is either an hourglass, pear shape, etc. I don't work this way as very few people have a perfect hourglass or pear-shaped figure. The top half of your body may be pear and the bottom may be hourglass. What you need to do is look at each section of your body from your neck down to your feet, step by step, and identify the assets and faults.

You are about to establish your own assets (yes, you do have them!) and faults. It is very difficult to look in a mirror and be objective as we tend to be far too critical about our bodies. But the mirror need not always be your enemy. Your aim is to highlight your assets and camouflage your faults – this you can and must do.

With the correct silhouettes to highlight your assets, I guarantee that by the end of this chapter you will feel and look slimmer.

Circle your assets and faults on the figure analysis chart. Once you have completed this easy exercise continue to the relevant section. For example, if you have wide hips, go to the section on 'hips' to see what you must and must not do.

There is a summary on page 26 which you should also complete for future reference.

## INDIVIDUAL FIGURE ANALYSIS

For an accurate analysis of your figure, this exercise should be done in front of a full-length mirror, preferably undressed. You will need to use a tape measure.

### NECK
Your neck should be half the length of your face. To determine this, measure the distance from the top of your forehead to your chin. Then measure the length of your neck, which is from your chin down to your collarbone. You can allow 2 cm (¾ in) either way for a balanced measurement.

*Short:*     Your neck is less than half.
*Long:*     Your neck is more than half.
*Balanced:*   Your neck is exactly half.

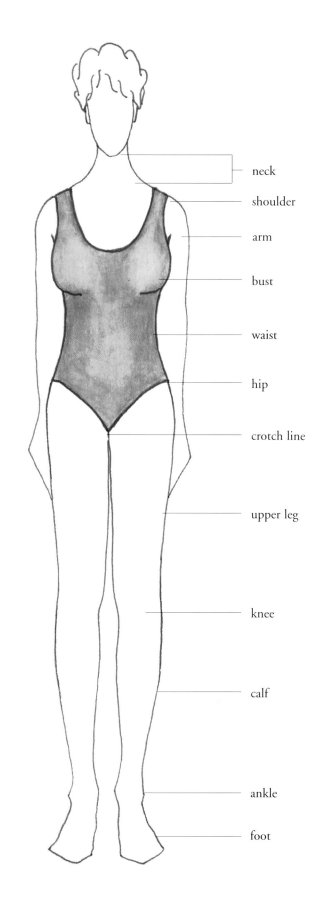

neck
shoulder
arm
bust
waist
hip
crotch line
upper leg
knee
calf
ankle
foot

## SHOULDERS

Stand up straight with your arms relaxed at your sides and compare the width of your shoulders with the width of your hips.

*Narrow:* Your shoulders are narrower than your hips.

*Wide:* Your shoulders are wider than your hips.

*Balanced:* Your shoulders and hips are in a straight line.

## ARMS

Stand up straight and relax your arms at your sides. Your arms are:

*Short:* If your elbows are above your waistline.

*Long:* If your elbows are below your waistline.

*Balanced:* If your elbows are in line with your waist.

## BUST

*Small:* Your bra cup size is A.

*Full:* Your bra cup is a size C or larger.

*Average:* Your bra cup size is B.

## WAIST (WIDTH)

Your natural waistline is in the gap between your last rib and hip bone.

*Small:* Your waist is much narrower (more than 15 cm/6 in) than your hips.

*None:* Your waist is exactly the same width as your hips and does not shape inwards.

*Average:* Your waist shapes in slightly.

## WAIST (LENGTH)

A balanced waistline is midway between your shoulders and the starting point of your legs (the crotch line).

*Short:* Your waist is less than halfway.

*Long:* Your waist is more than halfway.

*Balanced:* Your waist is halfway.

## STOMACH

Turn to your side.

*Flat:* Your stomach has no fullness.

*Rounded:* Your stomach has a slightly full shape to it.

*Full:* Your stomach extends quite far, especially further than the fullness of your bust.

## HIPS

Stand facing your mirror.

*Small:* Your hips are narrower than your shoulders.

*Wide:* Your hips are wider than your shoulders.

*Balanced:* Your hips are balanced or slightly wider than your shoulders.

## BOTTOM

Turn to your side.

*Flat:* Your bottom has no shape whatsoever and tends to droop.

*Full:* Your bottom extends quite far from your body.

*Average:* Your bottom extends slightly from your body.

## LEGS (1)

Measure from the top inside of your leg to the floor. The middle of your kneecap should be the halfway mark.

*Upper leg*

Shorter than bottom half of leg:

Yes          No

Longer than bottom half of leg:

Yes          No

Balanced – it is the same:

Yes          No

*Lower leg*

Shorter than top half of leg:

Yes          No

Longer than top half of leg:

Yes          No

Balanced – it is the same:

Yes          No

## LEGS (2)

To compare leg length versus total height, measure your body from shoulder to floor. The halfway point should be where your legs join the top half of your body (the crotch line).

*Short:* Your leg measurement is less than halfway.

*Long:* Your leg measurement is more than halfway.

*Balanced:* Your leg measurement is exactly halfway.

## KNEES

You need to establish if your knees are long, slim and shaped from north to south, or whether they have dimples or puffs and are shaped from east to west.

*Good:* No puffs or dimples.

*Bad:* Puffs, dimples, plenty of wrinkles, not firm.

*Average:* Not so bad.

## CALVES

To see the shape of your legs from the front, turn to face the mirror. To see the shape from the side turn both your feet outwards like a ballerina.

*Thin:* There is no shape at all.

*Full:* Your calves carry excess weight, retain water or are extremely muscular.

*Average:* Slight fullness.

## ANKLES

Turn to face the mirror.

*Thin:* Your ankles are very slim.

*Thick:* Your ankles are swollen or thick.

*Average:* Your ankles are tapered and well shaped.

## FEET

*Small:* Your shoe size is smaller than size 4.

*Big:* Your shoe size is larger than size 8.

*Average:* Your shoe size is between sizes 4 and 7.

## FIGURE ANALYSIS SUMMARY

| | | | |
|---|---|---|---|
| Neck | Short | Long | Balanced |
| Shoulders | Narrow | Wide | Balanced |
| Arms | Short | Long | Balanced |
| Bust | Small | Full | Average |
| Waist (width) | Small | None | Average |
| Waist (length) | Short | Long | Balanced |
| Stomach | Flat | Rounded | Full |
| Hips | Small | Wide | Balanced |
| Bottom | Flat | Full | Average |
| Legs (1) | | | |
| Upper leg | Short | Long | Balanced |
| Lower leg | Short | Long | Balanced |
| Legs (2) | Short | Long | Balanced |
| Knees | Good | Bad | Average |
| Calves | Thin | Full | Average |
| Ankles | Thin | Thick | Average |
| Feet | Small | Big | Average |

**Before:** *Chata demonstrates how an incorrect hemline can shorten and widen the calf.*

**After:** *The correct skirt length makes such a difference. Now her legs look long and shapely.*

*The best length for a short jacket is into the waist. This style looks wonderful with pants.*

## LENGTHS AND PROPORTIONS

Fashions come and go, hemlines rise and drop. If you are a follower of fashion, wear your hems short when the look is short and long when the look is long, but only if the style is right for you.

You may be wearing the right colour, style and fabric, but if the length and proportion of your outfit is incorrect for your height and shape you will not look your best. If you buy a garment that is the incorrect length, have it altered to fit before you wear it.

Before walking out the front door, you should do what I call the three-point turn. Stand in front of a mirror and check your appearance from the front, side and back. Only when you are happy with what you see can you walk out the front door.

## JACKET LENGTHS

### SHORT JACKET
This length is mostly referred to as a Chanel or bolero jacket. The length must end at your actual waistline or 4 cm (1½ in) below your waistband.

You can only wear this style if you have a flat tummy, good hips and a flat bottom.

### MEDIUM-LENGTH JACKET
This length must end just below the widest part of your hips.

You can only wear this style if the length suits your hip size.

### IMPORTANT
Take off your shoes when checking your correct lengths. If your proportion and legs look good without shoes, then imagine what they will look like with them.

*You can only wear a medium-length jacket if this length suits the size of your hips.*

*A long jacket is the most versatile length and hides a multitude of sins.*

## LONG JACKET

Everyone can wear a long jacket, but the length will vary for each individual.

In order to achieve the perfect balance, measure the distance from the top of your shoulder to your ankle. The length of your jacket must end exactly halfway. For example, if the measurement from shoulder to ankle is 150 cm (60 in), the ideal jacket length is 75 cm (30 in).

## SLEEVE LENGTHS

### CAP SLEEVES

These should extend just past the end of the roundness of your shoulder. Avoid this length if your upper arms are not firm.

### SHORT SLEEVES

Halfway between shoulder and elbow.

### ELBOW LENGTH

Just to the tip of the elbow bone.

### LONG SLEEVES

These should extend to the end of your wrist bone, no longer. If your sleeve ends at the widest part of your hand, it only makes your hands and, in turn, your hips look wider.

## LEG LENGTHS

When establishing your leg lengths, stand with your feet together and turn one leg out to the side so that you can see the shape of your legs from the front and side. Do the same exercise from the back so that you can check from behind.

### THIGH LENGTH (ABOVE THE KNEE)

Only wear this length if your legs and knees are slim and shapely.

**Before:** *Avoid hemlines that end directly on top of your kneecap.*

Ensure that no puffs, dimples or bulges show when you walk. Your hemline must end between 4–6 cm (1½–2¼ in) above the top of your kneecap. You can go higher if you wish, but keep in mind that your thigh will begin shaping outwards from that point. Remember that your skirt must fit you properly so that when you are dressed – especially if you have bad thighs or cellulite – your thighs don't show.

**After:** *Thigh-length skirts work best if they are 4–6 cm (1½–2¼ in) above the top of your kneecap.*

## KNEE LENGTH

Most women can wear this length. The question is – 'Where should your hemline end?'

If you had to jump up and down in front of the mirror without any clothes on, the only part of your body that is guaranteed not to move is from mid-knee down – quite a scary thought isn't it? With the correct knee length you will see only the lower and firmest part of your leg. If the lower half of your leg really doesn't allow you to wear this length, then don't.

Hold the hemline of a skirt at the worst point on your knee, just above the kneecap. To establish your best length slowly drop the hemline by sliding it down your kneecap until your puffs and dimples disappear, and until your hemline covers the lump at the back of the knee.

If your puffs disappear in the middle of your knee, then that is your best length, but if they only disappear at the bottom of your knee, then that is the correct length for you. If you don't have any puffs or dimples, lucky you, you can wear your hemline at any point on your knee.

As a comparison, stand in front of your mirror wearing the correct knee length skirt and hold a long skirt in front of you. Look at yourself from head to toe and then quickly whip away the longer skirt and look at the shorter one. What are the first words that come to mind? Younger? Slimmer? Taller? More in proportion? What does the rest of your leg say? Curvy... firm... shapely...? The illusion will be that the rest of your leg will look like that too.

Never wear your length 4–6 cm (1½–2¼ in) below the bottom of your knee because this will cause you to lose the 'waistline' of your leg and will make your legs appear thicker.

*The correct skirt length can hide a bad pair of knees and make your legs appear more shapely.*

Once you have established your knee length, you must wear every style (pencil skirt, walking shorts, dress) at the same length. It may seem as though I'm being particular, but when you look at your proportions you will see what a difference it makes to your weight and shape.

## CALF LENGTH

The correct length is at the bottom of your calf muscle. Most books tell you to wear this length in the middle of your calf. I say 'NO!' as this is the widest part of your leg from your knee down. When you walk, your hemline will cut across this part, creating the illusion that the rest of your leg is wide.

If you are shorter than 1.7 m (5 ft 6 in) you should avoid this length because the hemline is almost at ground level and will make you appear even shorter. Rather wear a longer jacket or top with a knee-length skirt. This will create height and your proportion will be balanced.

## ANKLE LENGTH

You can only wear an ankle-length skirt if you are taller than 1.7 m (5 ft 6 in). You can, however, wear a dress at this length as there is a continuous line from your shoulder to the ground, creating height and slimness.

However, when you wear a blouse tucked into an ankle length skirt it creates the impression of being short waisted. Never break this silhouette in half with a belt unless you are very tall and have a balanced or long waisted measurement.

### Tips

- Always wear a slight heel when wearing a calf or ankle length hemline, especially if you are short.
- Wear your darker colour at the bottom and your lighter colour at the top.
- If you want to look slimmer, avoid big prints on the bottom half of your outfit.

**Before:** *A top tucked into a long skirt will always make you look shorter and wider.*

**After:** *A longer top or jacket with a knee-length skirt will make you look taller and slimmer.*

**Before:** *A top tucked into a long skirt makes you look short waisted even if you're not.*

**After:** *You can wear an ankle-length dress even if you are short as if forms a continuous line.*

*Jeans look great with smart, flat leather shoes or boots, never with a court shoe.*

*Tailored pants can be worn with flat shoes or a smart shoe with a slight heel.*

## THE CORRECT PANTS LENGTHS

When trying on pants remember to take off your shoes. If the pants bunch around your ankle, it does not mean that you must wear a high heel, it means that the pants are too long.

Do not establish the correct length by ensuring the pants cover the back of your shoes. The length will only be correct for those particular shoes. Wear your pants at the bottom of your ankle bone. The hemline will therefore always cover the back of any shoe you wear. This applies to all styles except cigarette leg, French leg (Capri pants) which should be worn just above the ankle bone, or pedal pushers (three-quarter length pants) which should be worn at the bottom of the calf muscle.

AN IMPORTANT REMINDER
Once you have established your correct lengths, they will always apply to any style that you wear.

## STYLE ANALYSIS — THE DO'S AND DON'TS

There must be at least one outfit in your wardrobe that, whenever you wear it, people constantly comment on how slim you look while you haven't actually lost any weight. It's the right silhouette you are wearing that creates this illusion. The perfect shape hardly exists and I don't want you to put yourself under pressure to achieve a figure or style which is unattainable.

While there is always room for improvement, you must be realistic about your assets and your faults. I understand the agony of an over-generous bosom or badly shaped legs, but I know how to do something about them. By now you would have identified your assets. Use them, and never compromise with styles that highlight your faults! If short jackets are fashionable and they suit you, wear them, if they don't, don't wear them. Within each season there are always other styles from which to choose.

What is the first thing you are inclined to do with a part of your body that you don't like? Cover it up? If you do it correctly, that's great. But if you do it incorrectly, you may be hiding your assets at the same time. Follow these guidelines and take the stress out of dress.

The correct fit of your garment is vital. It is not unusual to be one size on the top half of your body and another size on the bottom. These days, most outfits are sold as separates so you have a choice of sizes.

If you are wearing a size 10 and it fits you correctly, you may actually look like you are wearing a size 8. However, if you are wearing a size 12 and it is too tight, you may look as though you are wearing a size 14. Therefore, if your waist is a size 10, your upper hip is a size 12 and your lower hip is a size 14, buy the size 14 and get the waist altered to fit.

Before moving on, it is time for a geography lesson. Your aim should be to avoid styles that go from east to west and to look for the ones that go from north to south.

To explain this concept more clearly I have included diagrams on the following page so that you can determine the differences between the two. There are ten reasons why the one looks taller and slimmer and the other looks shorter and wider.

Which is the correct one out of sketches A and B and what are the differences between them? First see if you can work out the differences by yourself, and only then confirm the answers.

**SKETCH A**

1. The length is perfectly balanced between shoulder and ankle.
2. There is continuity of colour, creating height.
3. The buttons go from north to south, creating a slimmer look.
4. The shoulder pads are balanced with the hips.
5. The jacket and skirt fabrics work together.
6. No pockets – the tummy and hips look slim.
7. The sleeves are slightly tapered, adding shape.
8. Deep V-neck, the line goes from north to south.
9. The waist is slightly tapered, creating shape.
10. The sleeves are the correct length.

**SKETCH B**

1. The jacket is too long and makes the figure look out of proportion.
2. The colour is split, cutting the body in half.
3. The buttons go from east to west, creating width.
4. The shoulder pads are too wide, creating width.
5. The jacket fabric is too heavy for the soft skirt.
6. Pockets – the eye is automatically drawn to the tummy and hips.
7. The sleeves are too bulky, adding weight to the body.
8. Wide collar, the line goes from east to west.
9. The box style takes shape away from the waist.
10. The sleeves are too long.

The magic word is 'alteration'. According to what I've just told you, if your tummy is your problem area you should not wear double-breasted jackets. However, if you already have one you can have it professionally altered into a single-breasted style.

If you try on a skirt that has a slit in the front which shows off your knees and these are not your best asset, you can stitch the slit closed to just below the knee. You will not be showing your knees but will be highlighting the shape of your calf instead.

If you see an outfit in a shop window which has a body stocking as part of the ensemble, don't be deterred if you don't like the body stocking. Shop with an eraser in your mind and rub out whatever you don't feel comfortable with. Look for an alternative; replace the body stocking with a camisole. The overall look will be the same.

Don't be wary of doing alterations. It may be a nuisance at times but it is worth the money and effort that you need to put into changing a button, shortening or lengthening a hemline, or taking out or adding shoulder pads. It will make a crucial difference to your overall appearance and will help boost your self-esteem.

For the balance of this chapter I will show you how to highlight your assets and camouflage your faults. All you need to do is go to the relevant section. For example, if you are unhappy with your hips, turn to the section on hips and it will show how to correct that problem area.

However, if I suggest that you do not wear bands across your hips, I mean *no bands whatsoever*! Not on the end of a jacket, no welt at the end of a jersey, no leather bomber jacket with a band, no sash tied across your body. It means no bands, irrelevant of the style.

## SHORT NECK

Your aim is to make your neck appear longer and slimmer.

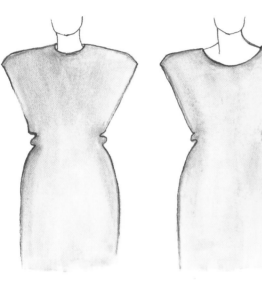   

✘
High, closed, round neck

✔
It is acceptable to wear a
round neck as long as
you can clearly see
your collarbone

✘
Polo neck

✔
Scooped neckline

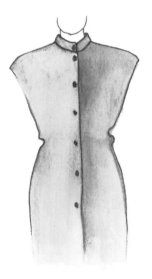 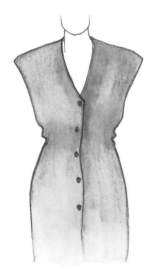

✘
Mandarin collar
and buttons done all
the way up

✔
V-neck or open shirt
Avoid chokers: See
necklaces (page 70)

## LONG NECK

Your aim is to make your neck appear slightly shorter.

Do the opposite of the above.

---

### Notes

- A high, closed, round neck or polo neck will make your neck look shorter.
- A Mandarin collar or buttons done all the way up will also shorten your neck.
- Avoid long, deep V-necks as this will make a long neck look even longer. A regular V-neck will work best.

# NARROW SHOULDERS

Your aim is give your shoulders more width and shape.

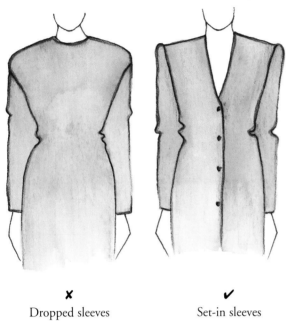

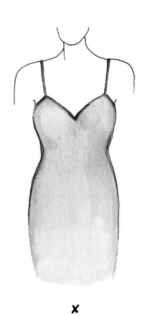

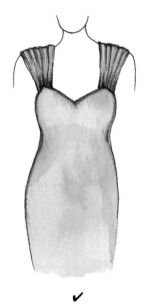

✘
Dropped sleeves

✔
Set-in sleeves

✘
Thin spaghetti straps

✔
Rouched straps to create
fullness, pleating, gauging

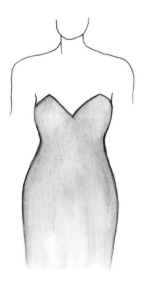

✘
Strapless

✔
Sweetheart neckline

## Tip

Shoulder pads create the illusion of having wider
shoulders. Ensure that your shoulder pads end at the
end of your own shoulder, then add darts, pleats or
gauging to make the shoulder look wider.

## WIDE SHOULDERS

Your aim is to narrow your shoulders yet retain the balance with your hips.

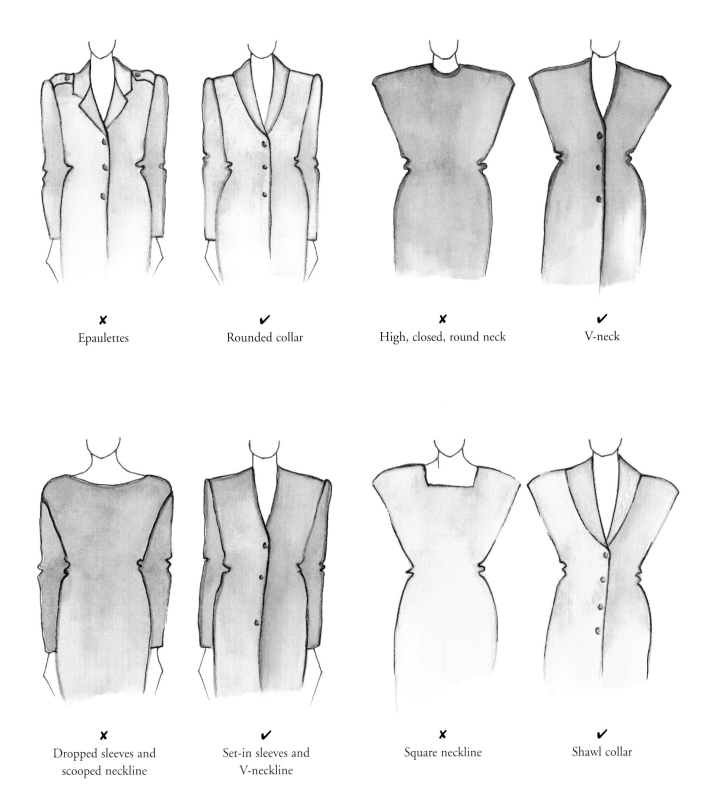

| ✗ | ✔ | ✗ | ✔ |
|---|---|---|---|
| Epaulettes | Rounded collar | High, closed, round neck | V-neck |

| ✗ | ✔ | ✗ | ✔ |
|---|---|---|---|
| Dropped sleeves and scooped neckline | Set-in sleeves and V-neckline | Square neckline | Shawl collar |

# WIDE SHOULDERS

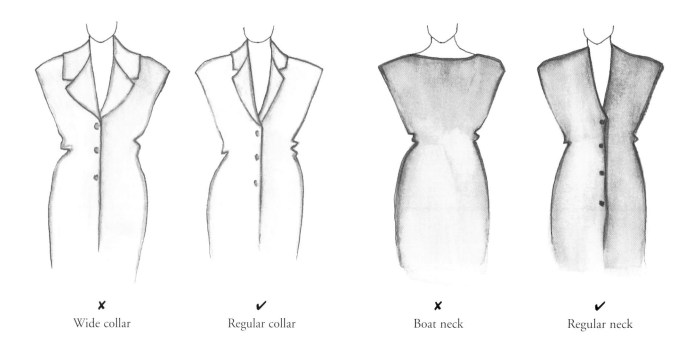

✗
Wide collar

✔
Regular collar

✗
Boat neck

✔
Regular neck

✗
Wide or excessively full
shoulder pads

✔
Set-in sleeves

---

### Notes

- Shoulder pads should end at the end of your own shoulder for the best fit.
- Avoid halter necks if you have wide shoulders.
- You should also avoid thin spaghetti straps. A strap 2–3 cm (¾–1¼ in) wide is more suitable.

## LONG ARMS

Your aim is to make your arms appear shorter or more in proportion with the rest of your body.

✗
Cap sleeves

✔
Wide cuffs and bracelets

✗
Sleeveless

✔
Short or long sleeves

## SHORT ARMS

Your aim is to make your arms appear longer but retain the balance with the rest of your body.

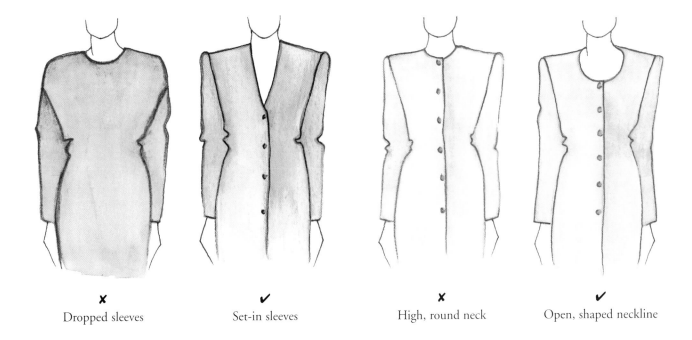

✗
Dropped sleeves

✔
Set-in sleeves

✗
High, round neck

✔
Open, shaped neckline

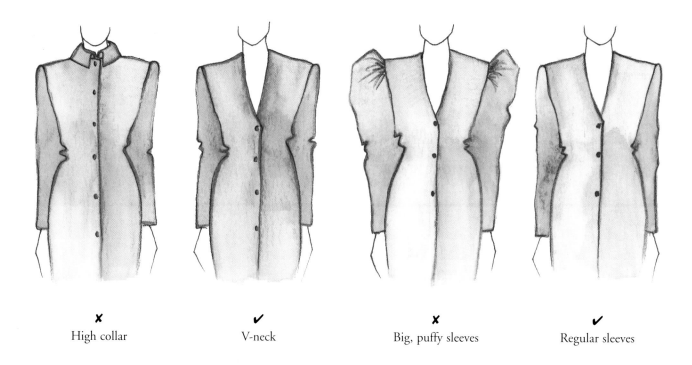

✘
High collar

✔
V-neck

✘
Big, puffy sleeves

✔
Regular sleeves

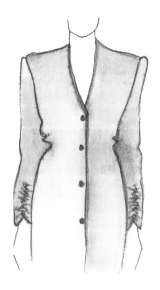

✘
Regular sleeves with
some rouching

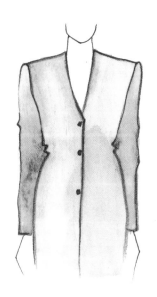

✔
Regular sleeves

Tips

Avoid any detail that will shorten the arm:
◆ Wide watches
◆ Lots of bracelets
◆ Wide cuffs

# SMALL BUST

Your aim is to make your bust appear fuller and more shapely.

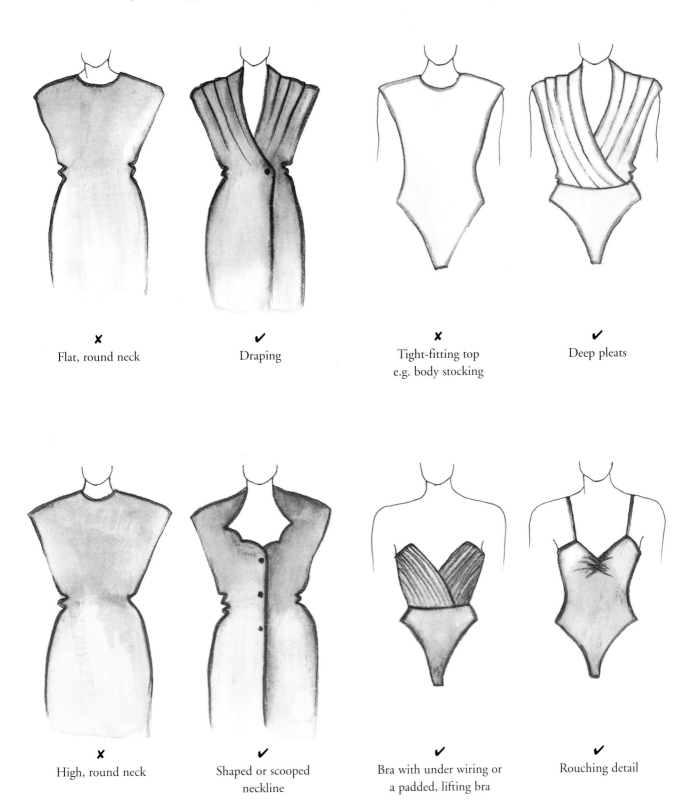

✘
Flat, round neck

✔
Draping

✘
Tight-fitting top
e.g. body stocking

✔
Deep pleats

✘
High, round neck

✔
Shaped or scooped
neckline

✔
Bra with under wiring or
a padded, lifting bra

✔
Rouching detail

# FULL BUST

Your aim is to reduce the fullness of your bust and to lift it.

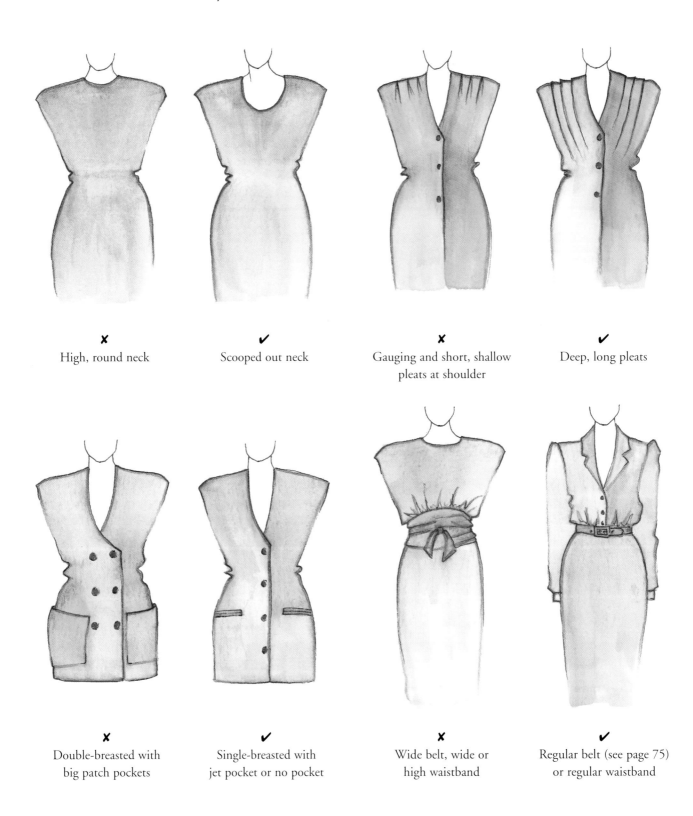

✘
High, round neck

✔
Scooped out neck

✘
Gauging and short, shallow
pleats at shoulder

✔
Deep, long pleats

✘
Double-breasted with
big patch pockets

✔
Single-breasted with
jet pocket or no pocket

✘
Wide belt, wide or
high waistband

✔
Regular belt (see page 75)
or regular waistband

# LONG WAISTED

Your main aim is to prevent your waist from appearing any longer. You need to shorten it but retain your proportion.

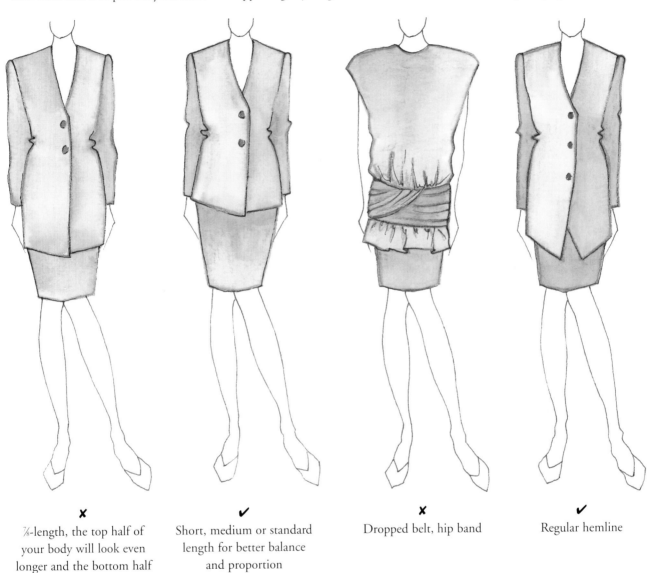

**✗**
⅞-length, the top half of your body will look even longer and the bottom half will appear shorter

**✔**
Short, medium or standard length for better balance and proportion

**✗**
Dropped belt, hip band

**✔**
Regular hemline

---

### Tip

Avoid very deep V-necks (the first button starts in line with your natural waistline) as this will make the top half of your body appear to be even longer. A short V-neck (the first button starts in the middle of your chest or in line with your bust) is more suitable.

---

# SHORT WAISTED

The aim is to make your waist look longer.

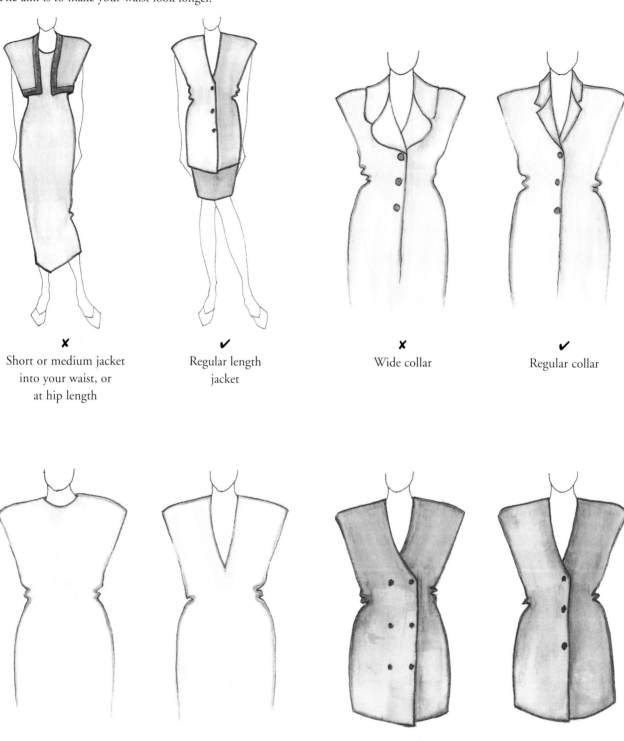

| | | | |
|:---:|:---:|:---:|:---:|
| ✗ | ✔ | ✗ | ✔ |
| Short or medium jacket into your waist, or at hip length | Regular length jacket | Wide collar | Regular collar |
| ✗ | ✔ | ✗ | ✔ |
| High, round neck | V-neck | Double-breasted | Single-breasted |

## SHORT WAISTED

✗
Wide belt

✔
Regular belt

Tips

Additional styles to avoid if you are short waisted:
- Wide waistbands
- Empire lines, where the seam is directly underneath your bust
- Horizontal stripes
- Big prints on the top half of your body
- High-waisted styles

## FULL STOMACH AND WIDE HIPS

Your aim is to make your tummy flatter and your hips slimmer.

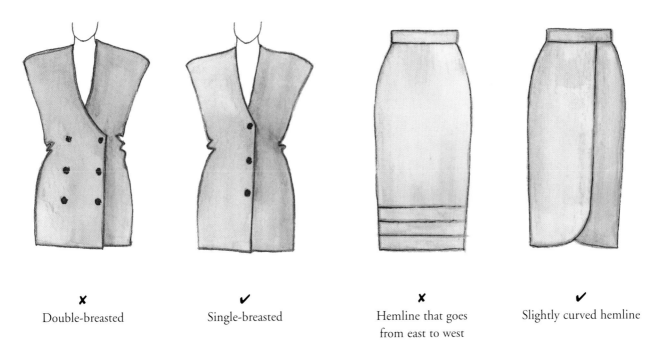

✗
Double-breasted

✔
Single-breasted

✗
Hemline that goes
from east to west

✔
Slightly curved hemline

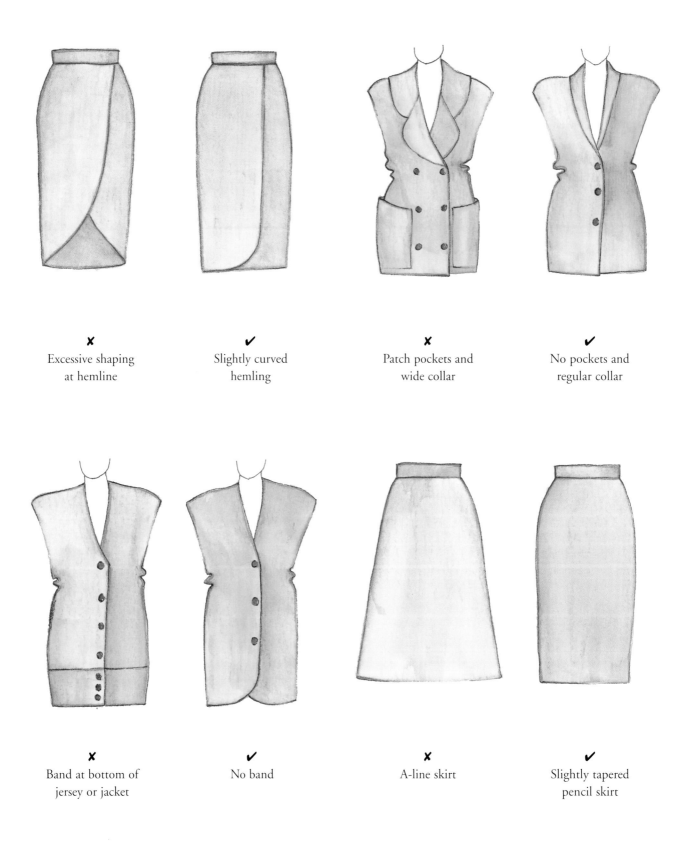

✗
Excessive shaping
at hemline

✔
Slightly curved
hemling

✗
Patch pockets and
wide collar

✔
No pockets and
regular collar

✗
Band at bottom of
jersey or jacket

✔
No band

✗
A-line skirt

✔
Slightly tapered
pencil skirt

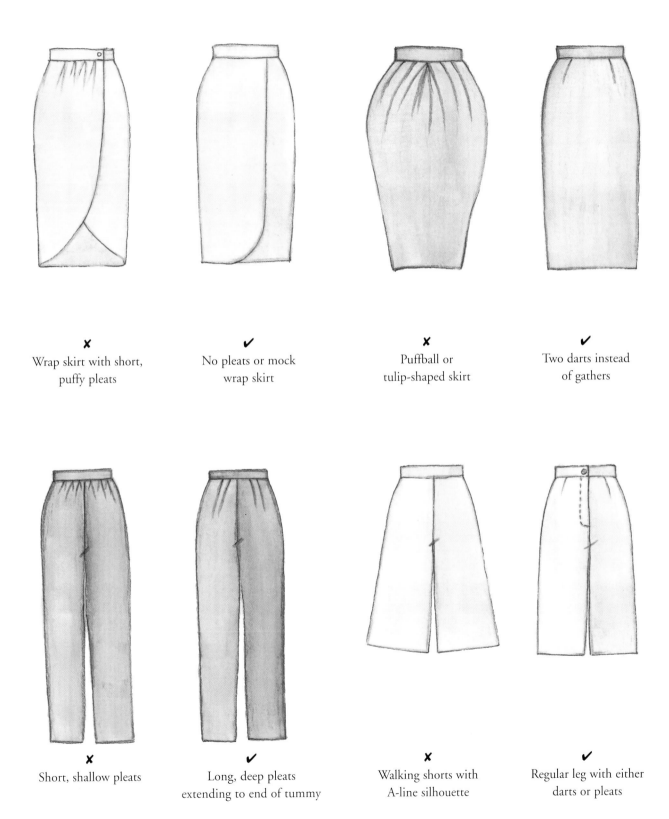

✗
Wrap skirt with short,
puffy pleats

✔
No pleats or mock
wrap skirt

✗
Puffball or
tulip-shaped skirt

✔
Two darts instead
of gathers

✗
Short, shallow pleats

✔
Long, deep pleats
extending to end of tummy

✗
Walking shorts with
A-line silhouette

✔
Regular leg with either
darts or pleats

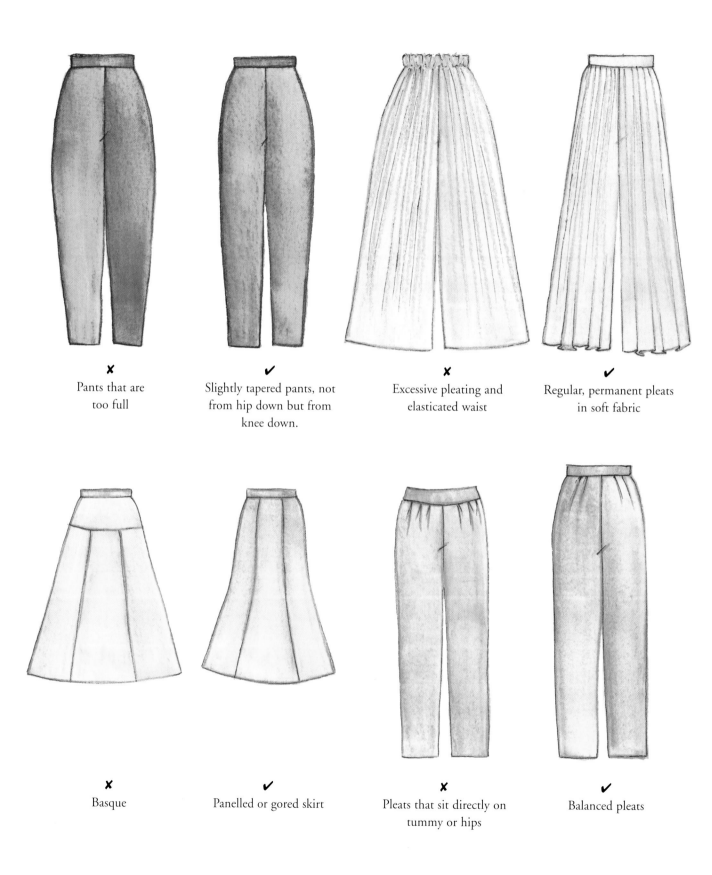

✗
Pants that are
too full

✔
Slightly tapered pants, not
from hip down but from
knee down.

✗
Excessive pleating and
elasticated waist

✔
Regular, permanent pleats
in soft fabric

✗
Basque

✔
Panelled or gored skirt

✗
Pleats that sit directly on
tummy or hips

✔
Balanced pleats

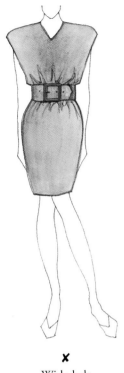

✗
Wide belt

✔
No belt – creates north
to south look

✗
Short jacket with
flared skirt

✔
Longer jacket/top over
flared skirt

✗
Top tucked into pleated
skirt with belt

✔
No belt, longer top over
pleated skirt

---

### Points to remember

- If you want to look taller and slimmer, wear styles with less detail.
- Invest in a full-length mirror.
- Never compromise on fashion trends – if a style does not suit you, don't buy it.

# SMALL HIPS AND NO WAIST

Your aim is to give yourself more of a waist.

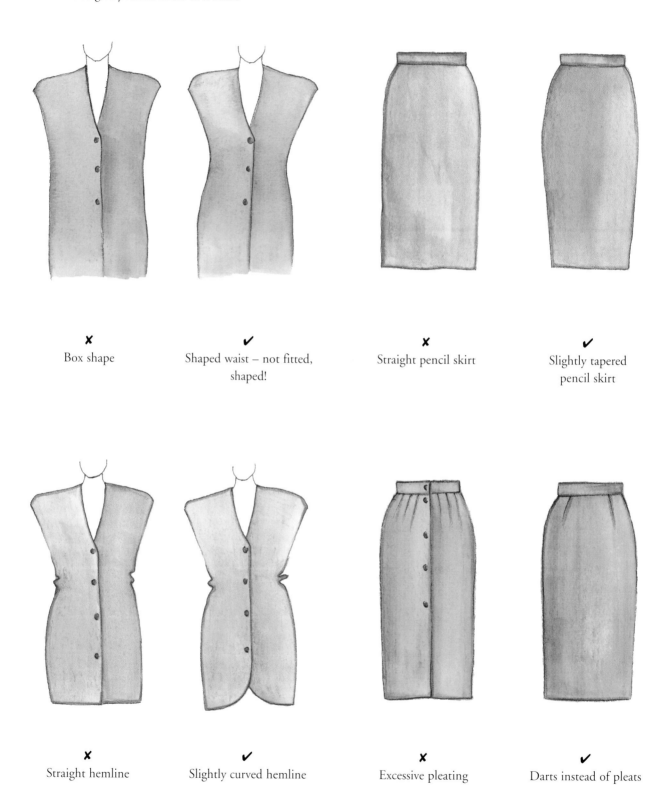

✘
Box shape

✔
Shaped waist – not fitted, shaped!

✘
Straight pencil skirt

✔
Slightly tapered pencil skirt

✘
Straight hemline

✔
Slightly curved hemline

✘
Excessive pleating

✔
Darts instead of pleats

## FLAT, LOW BOTTOM AND HOLLOW BACK

Your aim is to lift your bottom and, if very flat, make it appear slightly fuller.

<table>
<tr><td align="center">✗</td><td align="center">✔</td></tr>
<tr><td align="center">Style that dips underneath<br>your bottom</td><td align="center">Style that fits well,<br>removing all excess fabric</td></tr>
</table>

> **Tip**
>
> Pants can be altered to fit by unpicking the waistband, lifting the excess fabric back up into the waistband and stitching it up. Let someone who knows how to do this alteration help you.

## FULL BOTTOM

Your aim is to reduce the fullness of your bottom.

<table>
<tr><td align="center">✗</td><td align="center">✔</td><td align="center">✗</td><td align="center">✔</td></tr>
<tr><td align="center">Band</td><td align="center">No band</td><td align="center">Short jacket into<br>your waist.</td><td align="center">Longer length<br>jacket</td></tr>
</table>

# FULL BOTTOM

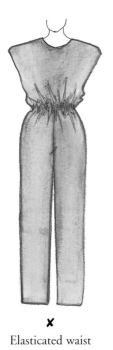

✗

Elasticated waist

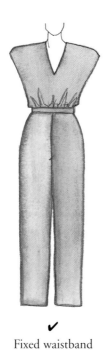

✔

Fixed waistband

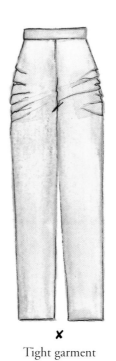

✗

Tight garment

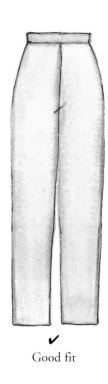

✔

Good fit

✗

Pleated skirt

✔

Panelled or gored skirt

---

### Tip

There are wonderful pantyhose on the market which lift and define the bottom. They give you an instant lift and make your bottom appear high, tight and perky – you'll never want to take them off!

# SHORT LEGS

Your aim is to lengthen your legs but also take your total proportion into consideration.

✘

An ankle-length skirt
makes you appear
even shorter

✔

Dresses are the
exception as they form
a continuous line

✘

If you are shorter than
1.7 m (5 ft 6 in) do not
wear ankle-length outfits,
they make you look shorter

✔

Wear a longer jacket over a
thigh-length skirt, but only
if your legs and knees
allow you to

✘

Pleating and full,
gathered style

✔

No pleating

✘

Turn-ups, at either knee
or ankle length

✔

No turn-ups

## SHORT LEGS

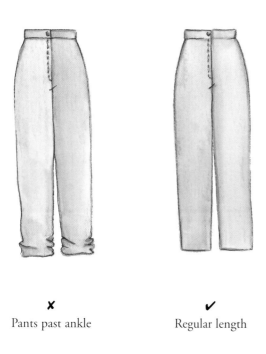

### Important guidelines

- Avoid fabrics that crease easily such as viscose, linen and cotton. Flannel, blended polywool and microfibre look and feel good.
- Do not wear tight pants – they should fit over the widest part of your body, namely your tummy or hips.
- If you want to look slim, do not wear trousers in bright colours and avoid any additional detail, such as elasticated waists or extra buttons.
- Always wear a belt with pants. This will add the final but essential touch.

✘
Pants past ankle

✔
Regular length

## LONG LEGS

What problem? Most woman would kill to have long legs. If your legs are much longer than your body and your waist is short, then your balance and proportion is crucial.

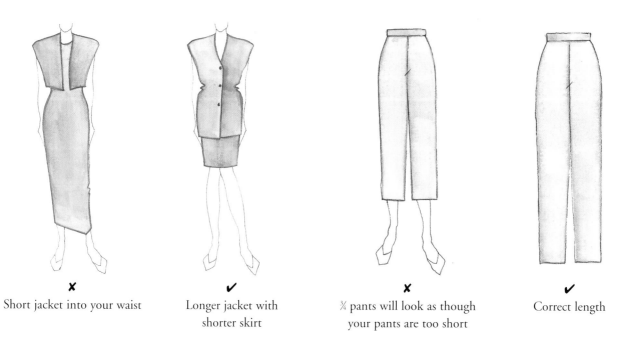

✘
Short jacket into your waist

✔
Longer jacket with shorter skirt

✘
¾ pants will look as though your pants are too short

✔
Correct length

## THIGHS

Your aim is to make your thighs disappear. The most important point to remember is that no one sees your thighs when you are dressed. If any item you are wearing is too tight it will not be very flattering, so the fit is vital. Do not wear skirts above your knees if they do not compliment your legs.

## KNEES

Your aim is to highlight your knees if they go from north to south, or conceal them if they go from east to west. Refer to the section on correct lengths (pages 28–30).

## ANKLES

The shoes you wear will play the biggest role here – see section on shoes (page 80).

## WIDE AND HEAVY CALVES

The aim is to make your calves appear slimmer and more shapely.

|  ✗  |  ✔  |  ✗  |  ✔  |
| Turn-ups at knee length | Avoid turn-ups | Double-breasted | Single-breasted |

# THIN CALVES

Your aim is to make your calves fuller and more shapely.

**✘** A-line skirt

**✔** Slightly tapered hemline

**✘** Very full, gathered skirt

**✔** Straight style

**✘** Turn-ups at knee length

**✔** No turn-ups

**✘** Double-breasted

**✔** Single-breasted

Invest in quality fabrics that last

# STUTTAFORDS

# FABRICS AND PRINTS

We often tend to focus on colours or styles and forget about the fabrics. Fabrics, however, play an important role in establishing the correct look and image.

The quality of the fabric is not determined by how much you pay for it, but by how versatile it is – the more costly the purchase, the more versatile it should be.

The personalities of the fabric and style must work hand in hand. A soft style needs to be in a soft fabric, and a tailored style needs to be in a structured fabric. Here are some examples which show the importance of using the right or wrong fabrics for a particular style:

- A pleated skirt in a soft fabric, such as georgette, chiffon or silk, drapes against and moves with your body. The same style in a heavier fabric, such as cotton or linen, would be rigid and would not move or drape against your body, thus appearing to add 5 kg (11 lb) to your weight.
- If you wear a tailored jacket in a soft fabric it will droop because the fabric is too soft for the style. The fabric must be more substantial, such as linen or polywool.
- If you tuck in a stiff cotton shirt and then blouson it over your waistband your waistline will blouson together with the waistband – even if you have a flat tummy, no hips and no bottom. Rather wear a shirt in a softer fabric so that when you blouson your shirt it drapes and falls against your body.

Fabrics with surface interest such as self-stripe, basket weave, Jacquard or dobby look great when worn with a plain outfit because they add an extra element of interest.

One tends to think that the reason a particular item looks good is because of its fit, but this is only one of the contributing factors – fabric has a lot to do with it too. A tailored pair of pants cannot be in a stiff fabric as it will not sit properly on your body. It also cannot be in a very soft fabric as it will sag in areas you don't want it to.

It is best to invest in practical machine-washable fabrics for daily wear, and high-maintenance fabrics for clothes you seldom wear.

For additional guidance, I have selected a few styles with a selection of fabrics that go well together:

**Soft styles:** Blouses, pleated skirts or draped/flared styles should be in silk, peach skin, crepe, viscose, georgette, jersey knit, organza, rayon, chiffon, silky Jacquard or microfibre.

**Semi-structured styles:** Unstructured jackets, shirts, pencil skirts, walking shorts or tailored pants should be in lightweight gaberdine, flannel, chambray, denim, linen, cotton or polywool.

**Structured styles:** Tailored jackets, pencil skirts and coats should be in wool, cashmere, boucle, grosgrain, melton, brocade, taffeta, tweed, twill, linen or gaberdine.

Some years ago, the rule was never to mix fabrics from different families, but today there are many that you can combine. For example, if you wear a woollen suit with a soft silk shirt underneath the overall look will be so much softer. Two different fabrics, one structured and one soft, when put together look great!

Fabrics from the same family, such as natural fabrics, can also be worn together. For example, linen trousers and a cotton shirt. However, there are some combinations that do not work together – a structured cotton shirt with a cotton knit skirt, or a T-shirt in knitted fabric with silk wrap skirt.

There is often some confusion between natural and man-made fabrics and which fabrics work together. Here are a few examples of the different types of fabrics that you can wear together.

*A lightweight cotton shirt with a polywool pencil skirt.*

*A lightweight linen jacket with a soft, pleated georgette skirt.*

*A viscose blouse can be combined with tailored flannel pants.*

*A soft, silky shirt can be worn underneath a flannel suit.*

*Woollen pants can be combined with a satin blouse for a softer look.*

## HOW TO LOOK AFTER FABRICS

◆ Always wash and hang dark colours inside out. This will prevent the colours from fading in the sun.

◆ Before washing, keep zips done up but undo all buttons. This will prevent damage to button holes and zips while garments are in the washing machine.

◆ To dry knitted garments, lay them flat on a towel. Do not hang them on a hanger to dry as they will stretch. You should do this with your T-shirts too.

◆ To prevent snags in pantihose and fragile items, wash them inside a pillowcase or special wash bag.

◆ Before drying shirts or items with collars, do up the buttons to prevent the collar from losing its shape.

◆ Use an iron cover to prevent shine on fabrics, especially when ironing dark colours and silky fabrics. If you do not have a cover, prevent shine by ironing over a slightly damp, lightweight cloth or hanky. Your best investment is a steamer. It steams out those little creases you cannot remove with an iron and is very useful when travelling.

◆ Hang garments upside down and peg them on the inside bottom of the garment. If you peg it at the top of the garment it often leaves marks that can be very difficult to iron out.

## PRINTS

◆ If you are overweight or shorter than 1.7 m (5 ft 2 in), avoid wearing big, bold prints. A useful guideline to follow is to check that the print does not exceed the size of your fist.

◆ To create the illusion of height, only wear prints on the top half of your body.

◆ To feel and look slimmer, ensure that the background colour of the print is always lighter than the print itself.

◆ Avoid stripes that are too wide and printed skirts that are long and flared.

**Before:** *If you are shorter than 1.7 m (5 ft 2 in), avoid wearing big, bold prints or stripes.*

**After:** *Brighter or lighter colours on the top half of your body will make you look taller and slimmer.*

STUTTAFORDS

## SWIM WEAR

When it comes to swim wear the most important aspect is choosing the most flattering style for your body shape. If you have a great figure, you certainly can wear a bikini, but bear in mind that very few of us look really good in this style. Here are a few guidelines to follow when looking for a bathing costume:

- Never try on swimming costumes in department stores' fitting rooms – those mirrors are deceptively unflattering. You end up trying on 20 styles and vowing never to eat another ice-cream.
- Medium leg flatters most figures – the best position of the panty line or cut of your costume is half-way between your waist and crotch line. A high-cut suits only those lucky few with no cellulite, puffs or dimples.
- If your tummy area is a problem, avoid a bikini. Rather wear a one-piece swimming costume.
- If you are skinny, avoid any strapless styles. Rouching, added frills, gauging or fine pleating will add an extra element of curve.
- If you have a heavy bust, choose styles with underwiring which offer support, and choose plains over prints. Avoid a high, round neck as this tends to make your bust appear fuller, opt for a lower neckline.
- Buy a swimsuit with a deep armhole. There is nothing more uncomfortable or irritating than a high-cut armhole which chaffs under your arms.
- If you are too shy to walk on the beach wearing only your costume, don't wrap your towel around you, it looks as though you are hiding something. Wrap a sarong or hip scarf around your body, or wear a lightweight shirt instead.

# STUTTAFORDS

## LINGERIE

We've come a long way since corsets. New fabrics have revolutionized the potential of underwear to enhance your assets and hide your flaws. Today we can choose from an endless variety of styles, and secret support comes in lingerie that ranges from smart and functional to sexy, with a delicacy that belies its firming effect.

Here are some tips for the perfect fit:

- Have your bust size measured professionally – it will save you both time and money. You should feel as though you are not even wearing a bra.
- The underwire bra defines the breasts by lifting and separating them; big busts look smaller and small ones look bigger.
- If cups wrinkle and pucker, try a smaller size.
- If the centrepiece does not lie in the middle of your bust and flat against your chest, go up one size.
- If the back rides up, the bra is either too big or too small. It should rest comfortably under your shoulder blades.
- The straps should be tight enough so that they do not slip off your shoulders but should not be so tight that they cut into your skin.
- Padded, lifting bras are favoured by small-busted women, as they lift the breasts to create cleavage. Ordinary padded bras increase your bust by one size and enhance the shape of your breasts.
- Lingerie has also become evening wear – a lacy bra can look very feminine and sexy worn underneath a tailored jacket.
- Lycra underwear gives you an instant tummy tuck, bottom lift and toned thighs without sweating for hours at the gym.

# CHAPTER THREE

# ACCESSORIES

*'Less is more'*
COCO CHANEL

ACCESSORIES CAN MAKE a basic outfit look outstanding or an outstanding outfit look completely wrong … it all depends on what you choose and how you use it.

Accessories are the finishing touches that personalize an outfit, update a wardrobe, or take a simple and versatile dress from day to evening and back again.

If your clothing budget is limited you can glamorize any outfit with some wonderful accessories. If it is not as limited, accessories can give you an infinite amount of chic and glamour, and make you look that much better for any occasion.

If you take an absolutely plain outfit, such as a white linen shirt and blue jeans, and add a beautiful leather belt with an interesting buckle, leather shoes and leather drawstring bag, you will have created an element of interest to your outfit and, although it is casual, overall you still look well groomed.

If you prefer a single strand of pearls and stud earrings, don't pile on the accessories as you will only feel uncomfortable. If you like the fun and razzmatazz of accessories, go ahead, but remember, when wearing a simple outfit, you can accessorize more. When wearing an outfit that is

heavily patterned, play down your accessories otherwise your overall look will be too busy.

I have emphasized the importance of proportions regarding body shape throughout this book; when it comes to accessories they are as important. In this chapter, you will discover which earrings suit the shape of your face, the correct necklace length, the correct shoe height for a particular outfit, some ideas on scarves, and more.

You certainly don't need countless different accessories. You should have a few items and add onto them as your budget allows. Remember to invest in good quality accessories.

# SCARVES

Scarves are primarily for winter but, depending on the fabric, can also be used in summer. If you are not a scarf person, don't wear them, but below are some new and versatile ideas you might like to try out.

## EXAMPLE 1

Take a square scarf (90 cm x 90 cm / 35 in x 35 in) and fold it into a triangle. Drape it over both shoulders so that the point at the back is slightly off centre – ensure that two-thirds is on your right shoulder and one-third is on your left shoulder.

Throw the longest side over one shoulder and secure it with a brooch.

For winter use soft draping fabrics such as wool, silk and cashmere, and in summer use chiffon or georgette.

*A silk scarf can be draped over your shoulders to create an element of interest to your outfit.*

## EXAMPLE 2
### (THIS CAN ONLY BE WORN UNDER A JACKET.)

Create a blouse! Take a rectangular scarf (30 cm x 1 m / 12 in x 40 in), drape it over the back of your neck and cross the left side over the right bust, and right side over the left bust. Secure the bottom of the scarf into the waistband of your skirt or trousers and you will have a beautiful blouse. Just make sure you are wearing a camisole or body stocking underneath so that if it gets hot you can take off your 'blouse'.

*A scarf can look like a blouse!*

*The 'blouse' effect is very versatile, especially if you do a lot of travelling.*

## EXAMPLE 3

Take a square hanky (30 cm x 30 cm / 12 in x 12 in) and fold it into a triangle. Fold again and gather the ends together as you would when putting a serviette into a glass. Pop it into a jacket pocket for that extra flair.

*Add a stylish pocket hanky for flair, elegance and a little pizzazz.*

## EXAMPLE 4

Take a square scarf (60 x 60 cm / 24 in x 24 in), fold it in half and then wrap it around your body. Secure the back either with a scarf clip or under the strap of your bra, put on a jacket, and you will look as though you are wearing a beautiful camisole underneath.

*Another great idea for the 'blouse' effect.*

Jewellery adds the finishing touch to every outfit.

# EARRINGS

ESTABLISHING THE SHAPE OF YOUR FACE

The best way to establish your face shape is to stand in front of a mirror with an old lipstick in your hand. Trace the outline of your face on the mirror with the lipstick. When you stand back you will see the outline of one of the following shapes: oval, sweetheart, round or square.

*Note*: You must not look at the shape of your eyes, nose or mouth, you must only look at the outline/shape of your face.

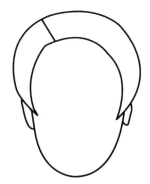

OVAL FACE (CHIN IS SLIGHTLY TAPERED)

An oval face is well balanced from cheekbone to jaw line.

This is the most versatile shape as almost any earring shape will suit you.

American Swiss

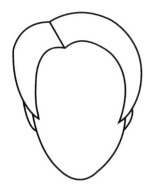

SWEETHEART FACE (HIGH, WIDE FOREHEAD, CHIN COMES TO A SHARP POINT)

A sweetheart face is short with a high forehead, wide cheekbones and full cheeks. The chin is sharply pointed and narrow.

You can wear any shape earrings except when the end of the earring comes to a point as this will accentuate the point of your chin. Avoid large, round earrings and thick hoops – fine or delicate silhouettes will work best.

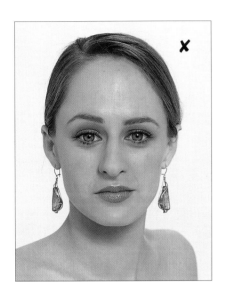

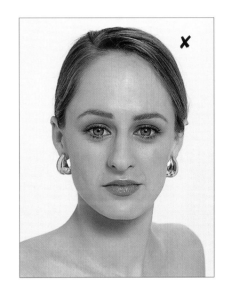

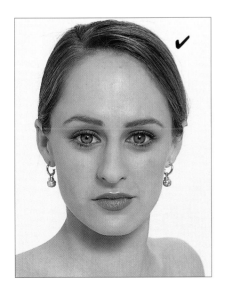

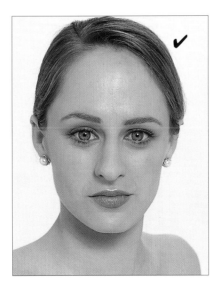

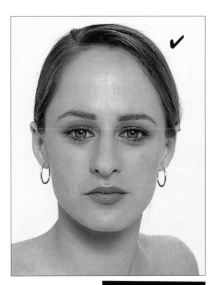

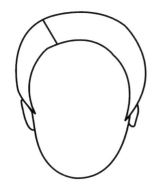

## ROUND FACE (CIRCULAR SHAPE)

A round face is soft, full, rather short and wide with roundness. Because of the cheeks' fullness and rounded chin, the bone structure is not very prominent. Avoid large round earrings as these will accentuate the fullness of your cheeks. A small round earring up to 2 cm (¾ inch) in diameter is acceptable. You can also wear oblong (egg-shape) or hoop earrings, as these will make your cheeks look slimmer and quite often eliminate a double chin.

As a test, put a round earring on one ear and a hoop earring on the other – compare both cheeks in the mirror. The round earring will give the shape of your face a rounder, puffier look, and the hoop earring will give more definition to your jaw line.

American Swiss

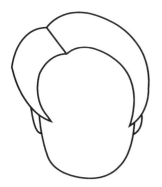

## SQUARE FACE (SQUARE, ESPECIALLY OVER CHEEKBONE AND CHIN AREA)

A square face is wide and short. The corner of the jaw line is symmetrical in shape and is strongly accentuated.

You can wear any shaped earrings except a square shape, as this will emphasize the squareness of your face.

Small oval or oblong earrings are best as they soften the jaw line, giving it more definition and shape. Hoop earrings are also an excellent choice. However, avoid large, chunky earrings in these shapes as they will make your face appear wider.

Round face

Square face

Oval face

Sweetheart face

Choose a style which suits the shape of your face

STUTTAFORDS

## GLASSES

Glasses can change your entire appearance – the bigger the size the more tired you look; the thicker the frame the older you look.

The main rule is actually very simple. Avoid wearing glasses that are the same shape as your face. For example, if you have a square-shaped face, don't wear square-shaped glasses. The one exception to the rule are oval glasses as these suit all face shapes.

The best way to establish the correct size is to ensure that the bottom of your glasses are in line with the bone that surrounds your eye socket.

*Before: Glasses that are too big can completely change the proportion of your face.*

*After: The right shape and size is very important, for both reading glasses and sunglasses.*

*Before: The incorrect shape can add years to your face – the thicker the frame, the older you look.*

*After: Contact lenses are the answer, especially if you have beautiful eyes.*

---

### Tips

◆ If you have a long, thin face look for frames that are slightly thicker as these will make your face seem slightly rounder and shorter. Avoid small, square styles.

◆ If you have a long nose avoid glasses that have high bridges, as these will create the illusion that your nose is even longer.

◆ If your eyes are set very close together do not choose a style with a large frame, as this will make you look as though you are a little squint.

◆ The middle of your eye should be in line with the centre of the lens to create the best proportion.

◆ Your glasses should be comfortable. In other words, if they pinch you they are too tight or if they slide down your nose they are too loose.

---

### OVAL FACE
Almost any style will suit you, but you must ensure that the glasses are the correct size.

### SWEETHEART FACE
Almost any style, but oval or slightly round is best.

### ROUND FACE
Avoid round glasses as these will make your cheeks appear fuller. Choose oval or cat's-eye shapes. Sometimes square shapes can work but be careful of these if you have a thin neck as they can make your neck appear even thinner and less shapely.

### SQUARE FACE
Avoid square shapes as these will emphasize the squareness of your face. Rather choose an oval or slightly rounded shape.

# NECKLACES

Make sure you wear the correct length with the correct neckline.

### SHORT NECKLACE/CHOKER
Do not wear this style with a high, closed round neck if you have a round face and short neck. This will make your neck seem shorter. Rather wear this style with an open neckline.

### LONG NECKLACE
The ideal length is halfway between your collarbone and the middle of your bust, or halfway from under your bust to your own waistline.

*Correct for long neck.*

*Correct for long neck.*

*Do not wear chokers if you have a short neck.*

*Rather go without a necklace for better proportion.*

*Incorrect for short neck.*

*Correct for short neck.*

ALL JEWELLERY SUPPLIED BY AMERICAN SWISS

# BRACELETS

If your hands are long and slim you can wear just about any style except very thin bracelets.

If you have short fingers and wide hands, avoid wide or very thin bracelets as they will make your hands appear even wider. A medium width bracelet will work best.

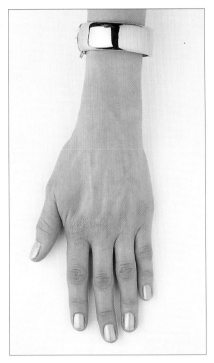

*Correct*

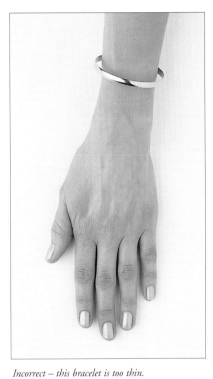

*Correct*

Incorrect – this bracelet is too thin.

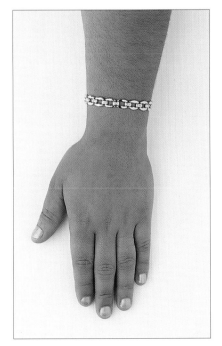

*Correct*

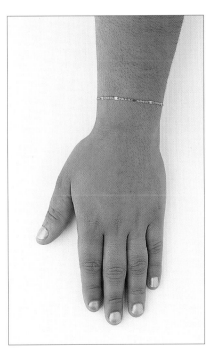

*Incorrect – this bracelet is too thin.*

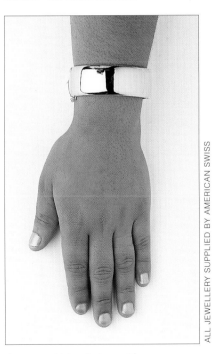

*Incorrect – this bracelet is too wide.*

# RINGS

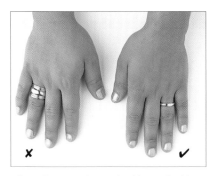

*If your fingers are short and stubby you should avoid wearing wide rings as this will make your fingers look even shorter.*

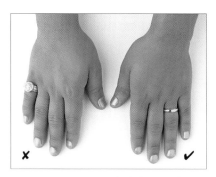

*Do not wear rings on your little fingers as these make your hands look wider because the attention is being pulled to the widest point.*

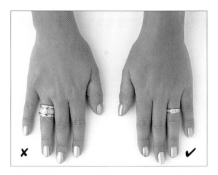

*If your fingers are short do not wear thick bands or clusters. Slimmer bands will elongate your fingers.*

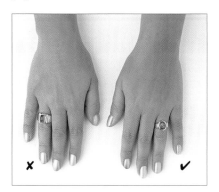

*Short fingers: Avoid big square shapes. Round shapes will make your fingers appear longer.*

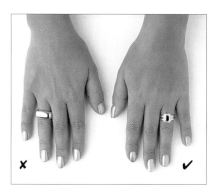

*Short fingers: Avoid wide bands. A small elevated square shape will lengthen your fingers.*

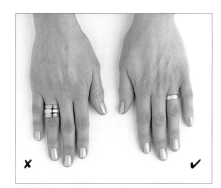

*Balanced fingers: To keep your fingers looking long and slim, wear thin rather than thick bands.*

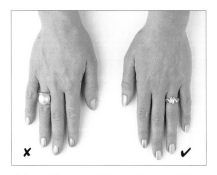

*Balanced fingers: Avoid shapes which extend from knuckle to knuckle as this uses up too much space.*

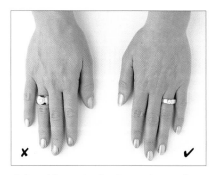

*Balanced fingers: Smaller, slimmer shapes will always keep your fingers in proportion.*

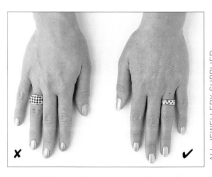

*Balanced fingers: Almost any ring shape will suit you, but avoid thick, wide bands.*

ALL JEWELLERY SUPPLIED BY AMERICAN SWISS

## Tip

Clean your rings regularly as soap often gets stuck underneath. Fill a glass with water, add a few drops of lemon juice and leave rings to soak overnight. Brush with an old toothbrush and see how they shine!

*If your watch slips past your wrist bone, your hand will seem shorter.*

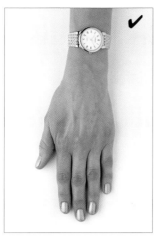

*The correct position for your watch is slightly above the wrist bone.*

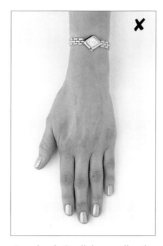

*Long hands: Small shapes will make your hand seem even longer.*

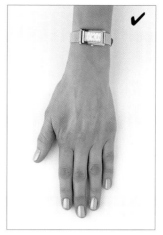

*Long hands: Rectangular shapes work best as they shorten your hand.*

*Balanced hands: Any watch style will suit your hand.*

*Balanced hands: A smaller face can look very elegant.*

*Balanced hands: An oval face is also a good shape.*

*Balanced hands: A rectangular shape will create balance.*

*Short hands: Large round shapes will make your hand appear fuller.*

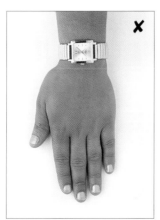

*Short hands: Large square shapes will shorten your hand.*

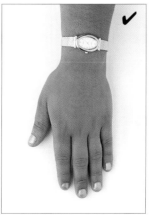

*Short hands: Small, oval shapes are slimming and look elegant.*

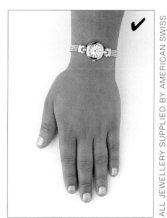

*Short hands: A bracelet watch looks dainty and lengthens your hand.*

ALL JEWELLERY SUPPLIED BY AMERICAN SWISS

Belts – an essential accessory

STUTTAFORDS

## BELTS

To establish which belt width is the best for you, you need to take the following measurements: Stand up straight and measure the distance from underneath your bust to your own waist, then deduct 5 cm (2 in) – this will give you the correct belt width. The reason you must deduct 5 cm (2 in) is to ensure that there is always enough distance from beneath your bust to the top of your belt.

### EXAMPLES

If your measurement is 9 cm (3½ in) and you deduct 5 cm (2 in) , this leaves you with 4 cm (1½ in). Therefore, 4 cm (1½ in) is the widest belt you can wear.

If your measurement is 5 cm or less it means you cannot wear a belt – this does not necessarily mean you are short waisted, you may just have a low bust!

Instead of wearing a belt, do one of the following:
- ◆ Avoid waistbands – the width of the waistband uses extra space.
- ◆ Don't tuck in. Rather wear a longer top over your skirt or pants.

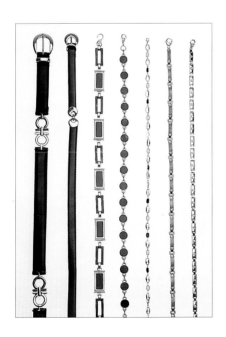

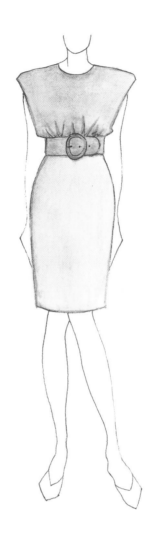

**SKETCH A**

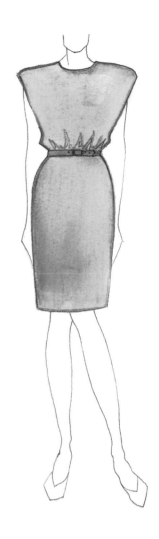

**SKETCH B**

Sketches A and B are the same. Example A has a very wide belt (8 cm / 3¼ in) and example B has a narrow belt (4 cm / 1½). Can you see what has happened to the proportion and balance?

1. The figure looks short waisted, even though it may be an illusion.

2. The bust line sits right on top of the belt, creating the illusion of having a drooping bust line.

3. The proportion and balance are distorted. The distance from the shoulder to the waist and from the waist to the knee is out of balance.

1. The length from shoulder to waist seems longer and in proportion.

2. The bust line appears to be higher and firmer.

3. The distance from the shoulder to the waist and from the waist to the knee and the knee to the ankle is now balanced.

## CO-ORDINATING COLOURS

The general rule is that you should never break your silhouette in half with a different coloured belt. For example, you should not wear a white top, navy bottom and red belt. Even if you matched up the red with shoes and a handbag, the belt will still cut you in half and you will lose continuity.

However, there are some exceptions. You can wear a white top, navy bottom and tan belt with tan shoes. Although the belt is not navy it is still within the basic family of colours and therefore blends together. A navy belt would also be suitable.

A bag for every occasion

STUTTAFORDS

*Basic, everyday smart bag.*

*Basic, everyday casual bag.*

*Classic evening bag.*

*Smart-casual bag.*

*Unless you are happy with your weight and body shape, your bag should never exceed the width of your body. However, if you have a full bust, tummy or wide hips, the wider the bag the fuller your body will appear to be.*

## BAGS

To ensure that you choose the correct bag length, stand sideways in front of a full-length mirror.

Wear a bag that creates a tall, slim look. Take a wide bag, turn sideways in front of your mirror and sling the bag over your shoulder. Now turn the bag so it goes from north to south and you will see that it makes your tummy and bottom look slimmer.

If you are short or have a problem with your tummy, hip or bottom area, avoid a long, envelope-shaped handbag. This style will emphasize the size of your tummy and bottom.

Do not wear a bag in line with your waist. It will throw out your proportions and make you look too short at the top and too long at the bottom.

You should also not wear a bag that reaches past the end of your bottom as this will make the top half of your body look too long and your legs very short. It could also possibly be sitting over the widest part of your body, being the lower part of your hips, which will emphasize your tummy and hips.

To create the perfect proportion, the centre of your bag must reach halfway between your shoulders and your ankle. Use the adjuster strap to correct the length. Alternatively, have the length altered at a leather shop.

Look for a versatile bag that will really work for you and which can be worn with a casual or formal outfit. It is not necessary to have more than 4–5 bags in your wardrobe.

## BRIEFCASES

The best styles are square, envelope or concertina in a good quality leather. Briefcases should be structured but soft and you should avoid heavy materials such as tin or metal, and very masculine styles.

The best colours for a briefcase are black, navy, tan or rust. Maroon and bottle green also look good but are not as versatile. Red is too flashy and if you are a businesswoman you will not be taken seriously.

*Invest in a classic, practical colour.*

*Clean, elegant silhouettes work best.*

**REMEMBER** Your attire can be impeccable from head to toe but if your briefcase looks battered and worn your overall image will suffer.

# SHOES

I have often seen women trying on shoes and quite obviously getting the heel height and hem length all muddled up. When trying on shoes that seem to be the wrong height, ask yourself the following question: Is it the shoe height or the hem length that is incorrect? To get it right, the first thing that you must do is determine your correct hemlines (see lengths and proportions, pages 27–31).

### GOLDEN SHOE RULES

- A good pair of shoes should last a few years and should not be worn day after day. This is particularly true of leather shoes. Leather 'breathes', so shoes should be put away for a day to air.
- Do not wear slingback shoes with pants – when you walk a little piece of heel shows from behind and does not look attractive. In addition, if you have short legs, your legs will look even shorter.
- Do not wear heels which are higher than 5 cm (2 in) with pants as this will make your legs appear to be completely out of proportion.
- If you have full calves, a slingback shoe is an ideal style for you. Put a court shoe on one foot and a slingback on the other as a direct comparison. Turn to the side in front of a mirror and look at the difference to the shape and fullness of your calf.
- If you have no shape to your calves the slingback is also excellent for you. It creates a marvellous shape.
- Do not wear a flat shoe with a knee-length pencil skirt. This will shorten the length of your leg and make your calf look heavier. A minimum heel height of 3 cm (1¼ in) is suitable. This style works well with jeans or tailored pants.

- If your leg is shapely enough to wear a thigh-length skirt, you can wear a flat shoe with it because 75% of the length of your leg will be showing.
- Use shoe trees to maintain the shape of your shoes when they are not being worn.
- Never delay shoe repairs. Reheel and resole shoes as soon as it becomes necessary.
- Never compromise on quality. Rather part with a little more money for a pair of good quality leather shoes than for plastic. Plastic does not last as long as leather so you will actually end up spending far more money.
- Have fun with your shoes. Compare, for example, a plain black shoe to a black shoe with a touch of gold, a two-tone shoe or some surface interest. Which shoe looks more expensive and interesting? The one with some interest of course.
- Do not wear white shoes with a dark hemline as this will make you look top heavy. I don't like white shoes because they get scuffed very easily and if you have a big foot, a white court shoe will make your foot look even bigger. White slingback shoes or sandals work well because the shoe is open.
- A flat-heeled boot is versatile and classic. When wearing a long skirt with a boot, the hemline must always cover the boot otherwise it will make your lower leg look too heavy, and can also make the boot or skirt look as though it is too short. Invest in a leather boot in a basic colour that will go with smart and casual outfits.
- Shoes with ankle straps shorten the leg and make the calf appear wider.

- When wearing an outfit in a bright colour (for example, orange or red) tone it down with two tone shoes.
- Regular polishing will keep leather supple and prevent cracking.
- If your legs are very slim be wary of stiletto heels as they will make your legs look even thinner.
- Never buy shoes when you are in a hurry or when your feet are swollen. Try on both shoes and walk around to ensure that they are comfortable.
- Trainers are an essential basic but only wear them with casual shorts, jeans or a tracksuit.
- If your legs are thick and heavy do not wear shoes with a spiky heel as the thinness of the heel will not complement the shape of your leg. Also avoid square-head heels. Rather wear a medium width heel.

### THE ESSENTIAL SHOES

- *Court shoes:* Can be worn with any style except casual clothes.
- *Slingbacks and sandals:* Can be worn with any style except winter pants.
- *Flat walking shoes:* Can be worn with any style except a pencil skirt.
- *Boots:* Can be worn with any style except a short skirt or soft dress.
- *Running shoes:* Should only be worn with shorts and tracksuits.

---

### Tip

Always keep your shoes in their original boxes as this prevents them from becoming dusty. Take a photograph of the shoe and put it on the front of the shoe box so that you can locate your shoes quickly.

---

Essential styles for every woman's wardrobe

STUTTAFORDS

*Pantyhose are a very important accessory and essential when wearing a suit.*

## PANTYHOSE

I once attended a presentation where, upon first impression, the guest speaker looked immaculate. She was standing behind a podium so I could only see her from the waist up. When she finished speaking and walked around the podium, I was shocked to see her shoes were very badly marked and she had a run in her pantyhose. This is, of course, unacceptable in the corporate environment. The moral of the story: invest in good quality shoes and always have a spare pair of pantyhose in your bag, especially if you are in the public eye.

Pantyhose are a must when wearing a suit with a court shoe. No matter what the weather, you will not look professional or well groomed unless you are wearing pantyhose.

Denier is the hosiery term for the density or weight of a pair of pantyhose. The lower the denier the finer the hose, the higher the denier the thicker and warmer the hose. A suitable denier for summer is 17, and a good weight for winter is 40.

Avoid wearing coloured pantyhose. When wearing a red suit, don't wear red pantyhose. They are too loud and flashy. Rather wear a neutral colour, for example ivory, Grecian blonde, blonde, nude, blackmail or French navy. A versatile colour is Mexican silver, which I simply love because it goes with almost everything.

Thick black opaque tights should only be worn with thigh-length skirts or under pants.

Don't wear patterned pantyhose with a printed outfit, as the prints will clash. If you like patterns only wear them with a plain outfit.

To prevent snagging, always turn your rings to face the inside of your hands when putting on pantyhose.

Pantyhose are an essential finishing touch for a well-groomed look

STUTTAFORDS

# CHAPTER FOUR

# TRUE OR FALSE?

*'The more you know, the less you need'*
ABORIGINAL SAYING

NOT EVERYONE CAN
WEAR BLACK.
*False.* Black is the easiest colour to
wear but it does depend on which
part of your body you wear it. Many
women are told by colour consultants
that they cannot wear black and have
banned it from their wardrobes! If
you have light colouring (blonde hair,
fair skin) do not wear a black polo
neck as it will seem to separate your
face from the rest of your body. It will
also make you look tired and will
drain the colour from your face. You
can wear it in a jacket, body stocking,
skirt, or pants, as long as it is away
from your face.

NATURAL FIBRES ARE
ALWAYS BEST.
*False.* Not any more. Man-made fabrics
have changed dramatically since the
days of Crimplene and nylon! New
fabrics 'breathe' while still being less
expensive and machine washable.
Microfibre is a new fabric that has the
same feel as viscose but does not crease
as easily, and Tactel is a nylon fibre
that has the feel and comfort of cotton.

ONE-COLOUR DRESSING
MAKES YOU LOOK TALLER.
*True.* It can make you look taller and
sometimes slimmer, especially if the
colour is a darker one. (To achieve the

same effect when wearing two colours,
always wear the lighter colour at the
top and a darker colour at the bottom,
as this creates an illusion of height.)

ALWAYS WEAR DARK COLOURS
IN WINTER AND BRIGHT OR
LIGHT COLOURS IN SUMMER.
*False.* Red looks good in a winter coat
and simply stunning with a tan in
summer. I believe it depends on the
individual's likes and dislikes, but just
because it is cold outside it doesn't
mean you must wear more subtle
colours. On the contrary, I would
eliminate the whole idea of separate
winter and summer wardrobes.

VERTICAL LINES ARE ALWAYS SLIMMING.

*False.* Vertical lines and narrow stripes do have a slimming effect because your eye travels from head to toe, but if the stripe is too wide it can also create width. Narrow stripes which are not set too close together are ideal. A straight skirt will deduct kilo's while a pleated skirt will add extra weight.

*If you want to look tall and slim avoid big prints on the bottom half of your body. Wear small prints on the top half and keep the bottom plain.*

*As you can see, if your shoe is lighter than your hemline your body loses proportion. Your shoe colour should match your hemline or be one shade darker.*

YOUR BAG AND SHOES SHOULD ALWAYS MATCH.

*True.* But there are exceptions. If you're wearing a navy skirt, you can wear a brown or a navy bag with brown shoes.

REAL STYLE NEVER DATES.

*True.* Classic silhouettes like a Chanel jacket, a good pair of jeans, a tailored pair of pants or a white shirt never date.

PREVIOUS YEARS' FASHIONS RETURN AND YOU CAN RECYCLE YOUR OLD CLOTHES.

*True and false.* Clothing does come back into fashion again, but when they do they may not suit you anymore. You will be older and possibly a different shape, so what suited you ten years ago may not suit you now.

*Certain styles, even when they come back into fashion, can look dated. Invest in a classic black or navy two-piece suit.*

WHITE SHOES ARE A GOOD BASIC.

*False.* White shoes only co-ordinate with a white outfit. You should avoid white shoes if your foot is larger than a size 3 as white can make your foot look even bigger. A white court shoe, as expensive as it may be, marks easily. The only styles in white which flatter your feet are a strappy summer sandal or slingback shoe. Darker, neutral colours like tan, brown, navy and black are the best basics to have in your wardrobe.

**LENGTH AND PROPORTION ARE VITAL.**

*True.* You can look taller and slimmer in a fraction of a second as long as your proportions are balanced. In the first photograph the woman looks very short waisted and her legs too long. The balance is very important.

**TUCKING IN MAKES YOU LOOK SLIMMER.**

*False.* To create a slimmer silhouette it is best to wear a longer top or blouse over a pencil skirt.

*Never wear a top tucked into a pleated skirt as it creates additional volume over your hips and tummy. Wear a longer top over a pleated skirt.*

*Avoid tops tucked into long skirts as this will make you look short waisted. Rather wear a longer top or jacket over skirts or shorts.*

**ANYONE CAN WEAR LEGGINGS.**

*False.* You need to have very toned, firm legs. Most people can wear ski pants, which are not as revealing as leggings.

**THE FIT OF A GARMENT IS THE MOST IMPORTANT ISSUE.**

*True.* It is very important. Your outfit must fit you front, side and back.

**YOU CAN WEAR JEANS AT ANY AGE.**

*True.* If you wear jeans with a white shirt, tailored blazer, leather belt and shoes you will look stunning. However, if you are in your seventies and wear jeans with a see-through blouse, no bra, biker boots and a cowboy hat, the look will be totally wrong.

**AN EXPENSIVE JACKET IS A GOOD INVESTMENT.**

*True.* A good quality jacket that fits you perfectly and can be dressed up and down is one of the best investments you can make. A single-breasted, longer length and collarless jacket is the most versatile, as you can wear it with a silk shirt and tailored pants during the day, and with a white T-shirt and jeans to movies over the weekend.

*Do not wear leggings if you don't have the body shape to do so. Wear a long top covering the hips and bottom or dress up your leggings with a smart jacket.*

ANYONE CAN WEAR BOOTS.
*True.* However, it does depend on what you wear with them. Ankle boots work well with jeans and pants but not with a short or pencil skirt. Long boots work with a long skirt but not with shorts. If you have stunning legs you can wear just about any style.

THE SIMPLER, THE BETTER.
*False.* A very plain outfit worn without accessories can sometimes look boring. Most of us need an accessory of some kind – a splash of lipstick, a stunning pair of earrings or a feminine scarf – to complete the picture.

*Make sure that your hemline covers your boot by at least ten centimetres. A pair of good quality boots is an excellent investment for winter.*

YOU CAN WEAR HEAVY SHOES WITH ANY OUTFIT.
*False.* In the photograph on the far left the shoes are too heavy for the pencil skirt and separate the feet from the rest of the body. They will only work with jeans or casual trousers.

THE COLOUR OF YOUR SHOES SHOULD ALWAYS MATCH YOUR HEMLINE.
*False.* If you are wearing navy walking shorts with a white shirt, you can wear tan shoes and a tan belt. However, if you are wearing a dark colour, such as black or navy, you cannot wear white court shoes.

YOU ALWAYS HAVE TO WEAR A BELT.
*False.* It is better to go without a belt when wearing a dress, especially if you are short waisted. The only exception is when you are wearing pants.

*Even if you have fantastic legs, avoid wearing heavy shoes with anything other than pants or jeans. A court shoe or slingback always looks good with a skirt.*

Don't buy impulsively – ask a professional sales consultant for advice

STUTTAFORDS

# CHAPTER FIVE

# LIFESTYLE

*'Discovering yourself is an adventure that, like great
journeys, requires attention, emotion and patience'*
CHATA ROMANO

HAVE YOU EVER been invited to a function where the dress code is 'Smart-casual', 'Casual-smart' or 'Elegantly casual', and you've had absolutely no idea what this means? In this chapter we will not only decipher the dress code dilemma once and for all, but we will also answer the many questions you may have asked yourself again and again, such as: Who am I? What kind of lifestyle do I have? What clothes will best suit my lifestyle? Am I over- or underdressed for the occasion? What kind of image do I want to project and how do I plan my wardrobe to suit my lifestyle?

## IDENTIFY YOUR LIFESTYLE

You need to work out your *actual* lifestyle, not the lifestyle you would like to lead. The four different lifestyles are:

SMART – business meeting, entertaining clients, interview;
SMART-CASUAL – dinner with friends, committee meeting, smart restaurant;
CASUAL-SMART – meeting a friend for lunch, shopping, taking the kids to school;
CASUAL – movies, school sports day, sightseeing tour on holiday.

Firstly, let's establish what the main differences are between the different dress codes.

For example, you are a working woman in a corporate company where the dress code is smart and you are allowed to wear tailored pants to work. You are married with two teenage children. During the week you don't go out in the evening, but on weekends you like to entertain casually at home and may go to a movie. You love gardening and often go away over weekends.

I have just described a smart-casual lifestyle – 70% of your lifestyle is smart (work) and 30% is casual (entertaining casually at home, weekends away, movies). If your wardrobe consists only of suits and high-heeled shoes and there are no jeans, casual shirts or semi-formal items, your clothes are incorrect for your lifestyle because you have ignored the casual aspect.

As another example, you are a farmer's wife collecting chicken eggs, feeding the ducks and bottling jams during the week. You go to church on Sundays, which is formal, and once in a while you go out to dinner at a smart restaurant.

This is a casual lifestyle – 90% casual and 10% smart. If your wardrobe consists only of T-shirts, shorts and jeans, your clothes are also incorrect because you have ignored the smart aspect of your lifestyle.

Read the rest of this chapter and decide which section best describes your actual lifestyle. You may very well fall into two different categories, and therefore your percentages may alter. A really good tip for the next six months is to fill in, at the end of each day, which lifestyle you fit into. Call it your 'Lifestyle Diary', and constantly check your actual lifestyle against that of your existing wardrobe. Do not fall into the trap of shopping for items that are wrong for your lifestyle just because you would like to wear them one day.

Your lifestyle may change over the years. Perhaps you were a working woman and are now a mother at home; you would need to alter your wardrobe accordingly.

You will now have a very good guideline to help you select the correct items for your individual lifestyle and / or occasions you are invited to attend. Under the section 'Wardrobe Planning' (pages 95–115), I have also given you visual examples of all the different lifestyles.

# Establish a dress code to suit your lifestyle

The following pages will assist you in identifying the lifestyle which is right for you, with an example of the type of outfit to be worn for each lifestyle.

## Smart

*Some career / lifestyle examples:*
Financial advisor, accountant, lawyer, bank manager, secretary or personal assistant to the MD of a corporate company, lecturer, human resource manager, liaison officer, training and presenting seminars to board of directors and companies.

### Your lifestyle
When you think of smart you don't think of jeans, walking shoes and a tracksuit, you think of a suit. As a working woman you should project a professional, confident and successful image, yet you must still look approachable. Even though most of your lifestyle is smart, don't forget about the casual aspect when planning your wardrobe – it may only be 10% because you work Monday to Saturday, but it is still part of your life. Therefore your lifestyle is probably 80–90% smart and 10–20% casual.

## Smart-casual

*Some career / lifestyle examples:*
Architect, air hostess, book-keeper, doctor, dentist, antique dealer, bank teller, art dealer, auctioneer, hotelier, estate agent, travel agent, teacher, computer consultant, psychiatrist.

### Your lifestyle
Smart-casual means that the overall look is more smart than casual – 70% of your outfit is smart and 30% is casual. This also means that although you may work for a corporate company it is not conservative – the look is smart but it is more relaxed. Your true lifestyle, therefore, is a combination of smart and casual; 50–70% smart and 30–50% casual.

## Casual-smart

*Some career / lifestyle examples:*
Graphic artist, beautician, caterer, drama teacher, actor, clothing designer, pharmacist, optometrist, librarian, physiotherapist, advertising executive, theatrical agent, occupational therapist, nutritionist, reflexologist.

### Your lifestyle
Your lifestyle is more casual, yet you need to look well groomed. Therefore, 70% of your wardrobe is casual and 30% is smart.

## Casual

*Some career / lifestyle examples:*
Gardener, potter, home executive, farmer, animal breeder, nursery-school teacher, baby-sitter, textiles manufacturer, baker, dancer, waitress, student, hairdresser, musician, artist, landscaper, mother at home, gym instructor.

### Your lifestyle
When you think of casual you think of jeans and comfortable clothing. However, you may go out to smart restaurants and attend social functions, so don't forget that you will require some smart clothing. Your wardrobe should be 90% casual and 10% smart.

*Smart*

*Smart-casual*

*Casual-smart*

*Casual*

# CHAPTER SIX

# WARDROBE PLANNING

*'I wanted to create a style that would make you want
to eat the person in front of you'*
JEAN PAUL GAULTIER

I WOULD LIKE you to remember this chapter as my 'Chicken Mayonnaise Sandwich' story.

To make a chicken mayonnaise sandwich there are three ingredients which you cannot do without: the bread, the chicken and the mayonnaise. The same principle applies to your wardrobe. Without the correct colours, style and proportions you will never have a wardrobe that will work for you.

At present, there may be all sorts of problems in your wardrobe. In this chapter I will highlight them for you so that you can identify where you have been going wrong.

Most of us feel confident when we have a wardrobe full of clothes, because psychologically it seems as though we have a lot to wear … but the critical question is, does your wardrobe give you what you want?

You may be spending a fortune on clothes, yet never seem to have anything to wear. It is most probably because very few items in your wardrobe co-ordinate.

You can have 40 different items of clothing in all the correct basic colours, but you will end up looking the same every day. So your wardrobe must not consist of 90% basics, nor should 90% of it be fashion items.

The trick is to work with a few items in different colours, styles and fabrics that will all co-ordinate with one another.

Imagine I gave you a blank cheque with a limitless budget to replace your entire wardrobe. There may be some items in your wardrobe that you really love and wouldn't want to replace, but my point is that you have the opportunity to replace 100% of your wardrobe. As a percentage, how much of your existing wardrobe would you keep? If your answer is 25% this means that you only feel confident and happy wearing 25% of your wardrobe.

How much of your wardrobe do you wear regularly? It is impossible to wear 100% of it on a regular basis, because, for example, a floral top does not go with a checked skirt. You should be able to wear 70% on a regular basis. The other 30% should be fashionable items, evening wear and so on.

The following is a guideline of what percentage of your wardrobe should be basic, and fashion:

- *50% basics:* A red blazer or cardigan is a basic. If you bought a black-and-white spotted blouse three years ago or today it is also a basic.
- *30% fashionable basics:* Perhaps coral is the colour for the season and you bought a linen shirt. It is fashionable for that season but will become a basic / fashion afterwards, because coral doesn't really date.
- *20% fashion:* This is fashion that will only last for a maximum of 2–6 months. It is important to constantly update your wardrobe, whether it is with a top, a bottom, a scarf, or trim on a shoe. You never want to have to say 'I feel dowdy', or 'I feel frumpy'. Remember that trends are there to be used, but not to be followed religiously. So add a little fashion into your wardrobe each season, but make sure that the fashionable items you buy are the right style and colour for you and that they suit your lifestyle. It is pointless buying a bottle green skirt with a black and purple shirt if these colours are completely wrong for you. Don't shop impulsively!

## THE WARDROBE PLANNING CAPSULE

Now that you have established your best proportions, colours and styles, let's go into your wardrobe and start putting it together so that you can wake up every morning with the knowledge that no matter what happens during the day, you will always be ready for the occasion – on time! The real secret to correct wardrobe planning is simple: first analyze what you have in your existing wardrobe by using the wardrobe planning capsule provided on page 97. Then make a list of what you need and only then go out and buy the missing items.

Before you can create your personal wardrobe planning capsule, you need to understand the differences between hot, cold, basic and light colours.

*Hot colours* (warm colours): red, peach, pumpkin, purple, lilac, coral, yellow, pink, burgundy.
*Cold colours* (cool colours): blue, teal, emerald, turquoise, apple green, aqua, midnight blue, mint, bottle green.
*Basic colours* (dark neutrals): navy, black, grey, brown, stone, tan.
*Light colours* (light neutrals): white, winter white, ivory, cream.

Now enter into your capsule *only those items that are right for you* from your existing wardrobe, entering each item in the correct colour column. For example:
*Coral silk blouse:* Coral is a hot colour and the description of style goes under tops.
*Green jacket:* Green is a cold colour and the description is jacket.
*Navy pants:* Navy is a basic colour and the description is pants.
*White shirt:* White is a light colour and the description is tops.

Once you have completed updating your wardrobe planning capsule you will have a plan on which to build according to your actual lifestyle.

You should have a selection of hot, cold, basic and light colours. If you find, after filling in your chart, that you have three black jackets, two navy jackets and three brown ones, you will realize that you only have basic colours and no hot and cold colours to make your wardrobe look different. You can now go shopping with a clear idea of what you need, and can purchase the correct missing items.

GOLDEN TIPS ON WARDROBE PLANNING

- Do not duplicate. Choose one basic colour such as black or navy.
- Buy different styles and silhouettes.
- Remember to buy five tops for every one bottom.
- It is far easier to work around your print. Have you ever taken three plain colours and tried to find a print to match them? Rather work with the print and pick up the plain colours from there. Make sure that you pick up the strongest colours. If the print has mango, apple green and yellow in it, it is not going to go with a plain cerise or turquoise, but it will go with apple green.
- A guideline for plains versus prints: Have 70–80% plains and 30–20% prints in your wardrobe. If you find this difficult because you love prints, wear prints in the form of scarves or pocket hankies. Different printed tops and bottoms do not go together and will restrict the combinations you can make.

You can now build onto this foundation. Each item you purchase must go with at least three other items in your existing wardrobe that are right for you. Imagine you have 30 items and each of them can match up with three other outfits – you have 90 completely different combinations! This is what I mean when I talk about a versatile wardrobe.

If apple green is fashionable for a particular season and you don't like apple green or it doesn't suit you, no one says you have to buy it. Look at different options and change the example. Use emerald green or bottle green instead. Both of them look equally good with a navy bottom.

If emerald green is mixed with purple as a seasonal colour combination and it frightens you, leave out the purple and replace it with navy or another basic colour.

When building your basic foundation, try to use the total lifestyle concept, which accommodates both formal and casual wear. You will always need something for a smart occasion, even if you lead a casual lifestyle, and vice versa. Don't have a section in your wardrobe for 'Smart' and a section for 'Casual'. Each item may come from a different lifestyle group but when co-ordinated they look great.

## PERSONAL WARDROBE PLANNING CAPSULE

Use this example to update your existing wardrobe and see where the gaps are.

| DESCRIPTION | HOT COLOUR | COLD COLOUR | BASIC COLOUR | LIGHT COLOUR |
|---|---|---|---|---|
| Jackets | | Green jacket | | |
| Cardigans | | | | |
| Coats | | | | |
| Tops | Coral blouse | | | White shirt |
| Skirts | | | | |
| Pants | | | Navy pants | |

# MIX AND MATCH

Each item that you purchase should co-ordinate with at least three other items in your existing wardrobe. There is no point in saying that a navy blazer will go with your navy pencil skirt, navy pants and navy pleated skirt. They are all navy and you will look the same day in and day out.

See which of the following you actually do.

**Scenario A**

You wear a red jacket and mix and match it with six different bottoms and tops and look the same every day.

**Scenario B**

You wear a basic bottom, for example a black pencil skirt, and mix and match it with six different tops and look completely different every day.

In both scenarios you are mixing and matching a total of seven items, but the first example is incorrect. People are either going to think you love your red jacket or that you have nothing else to wear. However, in scenario B, because the top half of your body looks different every day, you will look different every day. No one will really notice the black pencil skirt.

Most errors are made by having too many bottoms and very few tops. You should actually have five tops for every one bottom. People tend to pay more attention to what you wear on the top half of your body and will not notice what you are wearing on the bottom half.

Divide your wardrobe so that the tops are on the one side and the bottoms are on the other – this way you can always gauge if your percentages are correct.

Strive to reach the point where you close your eyes, open your cupboards, and only then decide what you are going to wear that day.

Remember, only 70% of your wardrobe has to co-ordinate, so you can have some garments that do not go with anything else. Whenever you go shopping, keep those outfits at the back of your mind and think of ways to build onto them so that more items in your wardrobe will co-ordinate.

I have worked out a formula which shows you how to get 36 completely different outfits using only ten garments. However, so that you will understand the formula I have given you an example where none of the garments will co-ordinate because I have created all sorts of problems that you may have experienced before. In the second example everything co-ordinates beautifully.

You will obviously have more than ten garments in your wardrobe but I want to prove that you can work with the minimum to achieve the maximum. I will point out all the mistakes in the first example and then you can compare it with the correct example. Pick any combination from the first example and you will notice that none of them is correct.

*Incorrect combination: 4–10*

*Incorrect combination: 1–6–8*

*Incorrect combination: 3–6–7*

*Incorrect combination: 2–5–10*

The main problems are:
- Navy and black do not go together.
- You need to choose a single basic colour on which to build. If you bought a watermelon blouse in July and you look for a watermelon bottom to match in September,

what are your chances of finding the same colour? Almost zero! Buy both the top and bottom at the same time. If you cannot afford to buy both, don't compromise, rather wait until you can.

- There are too many prints in this capsule. The floral and spotted tops do not go with the printed skirts. You cannot mix and match prints but you can mix and match plains or prints with plains.

# EXAMPLE OF INCORRECT MIX & MATCH CAPSULE

1 JACKET

2 JACKET

3 JACKET

4 TOP

5 TOP

6 TOP

7 BOTTOM

8 BOTTOM

9 BOTTOM

10 BOTTOM

MIX & MATCH
COMBINATIONS

1 - 4 - 7
1 - 4 - 8
1 - 4 - 9
1 - 4 - 10
1 - 5 - 7
1 - 5 - 8
1 - 5 - 9
1 - 5 - 10
1 - 6 - 7
1 - 6 - 8
1 - 6 - 9
1 - 6 - 10
2 - 4 - 7
2 - 4 - 8
2 - 4 - 9
2 - 4 - 10
2 - 5 - 7
2 - 5 - 8
2 - 5 - 9
2 - 5 - 10
2 - 6 - 7
2 - 6 - 8
2 - 6 - 9
2 - 6 - 10
3 - 4 - 7
3 - 4 - 8
3 - 4 - 9
3 - 4 - 10
3 - 5 - 7
3 - 5 - 8
3 - 5 - 9
3 - 5 - 10
3 - 6 - 7
3 - 6 - 8
3 - 6 - 9
3 - 6 - 10

Here, I have selected ten garments and the aim is to have 36 different outfits. I have also planned it to suit all occasions from smart to casual.

Pick any combination from the correct mix and match capsule and see if you come up with a co-ordinated outfit.

The advantages of having a well-organized wardrobe:

◆ You can select almost any combination to create a completely different outfit.
◆ All the colours co-ordinate with one another. Choose one colour from each of your four colour categories, and it will match up with any of the others.
◆ You can dress for any function in a flash.
◆ It is cost-effective as no garments hang, un-used in your wardrobe.
◆ You can work with the minimum to achieve the maximum.
◆ It eliminates the frustrating question of 'What am I going to wear today?'.
◆ You will know exactly what you have in your wardrobe and shopping will become a pleasure.
◆ It will eliminate impulsive buying.

---

Tip

First analyze what you have in your wardrobe, then make a list of what you need, and only then go out and buy the missing items.

---

*Correct combination: 2-6-7*

*Correct combination: 1-6-10*

*Correct combination: 3-5-9*

*Correct combination: 5-8*

# EXAMPLE OF CORRECT MIX & MATCH CAPSULE

1 JACKET

2 JACKET

3 JACKET

4 TOP

5 TOP

6 TOP

7 BOTTOM

8 BOTTOM

9 BOTTOM

10 BOTTOM

MIX & MATCH
COMBINATIONS

1-4-7
1-4-8
1-4-9
1-4-10
1-5-7
1-5-8
1-5-9
1-5-10
1-6-7
1-6-8
1-6-9
1-6-10
2-4-7
2-4-8
2-4-9
2-4-10
2-5-7
2-5-8
2-5-9
2-5-10
2-6-7
2-6-8
2-6-9
2-6-10
3-4-7
3-4-8
3-4-9
3-4-10
3-5-7
3-5-8
3-5-9
3-5-10
3-6-7
3-6-8
3-6-9
3-6-10

A versatile wardrobe where colour, style and fabric co-ordinate

STUTTAFORDS

## GET YOUR WARDROBE STRAIGHT

Follow these important guidelines when planning your wardrobe:

- 80% of your wardrobe should consist of items you wear on the top half of your body, for example blouses, shirts, jackets, jerseys and T-shirts.
- 20% of your wardrobe should consist of items you wear on the bottom half of your body, such as skirts, pants, shorts and jeans.
- It is far more versatile to mix and match separates than dresses, so try to limit the number of dresses in your wardrobe. Wear a top and a skirt that together look like a dress, but can also be co-ordinated with other items in your wardrobe. It will not only save you money, but will give you a more versatile wardrobe with which to work.
- One garment per hanger. This way you can see what you actually have. When buying an outfit don't put the top and bottom on the same hanger. If you hang them separately you will be able to co-ordinate them with other items instead of only wearing them together.
- Don't use wire hangers as these ruin the shape of your garments and cause them to crease. If you live near the sea, wire hangers may rust and stain your clothes. Rather use wooden or even good quality plastic hangers.
- Don't jam everything you own into your wardrobe. Make sure you can see all that you have, or at least most of what you own. It makes it so much easier to decide on an outfit, whatever the occasion. Nothing is more frustrating than pulling out a crumpled shirt which you'll have to spend time ironing before you can wear it.
- Never hang knitwear as it will stretch and lose its shape. Always fold jerseys and knitted items.
- Use drawers for underwear, socks, gloves and pantyhose. Ideally use transparent containers so you can easily see what you have.
- Don't just throw out the clothes you don't want. Give them to charities, second-hand shops or the Salvation Army. They really do appreciate it and your clothes will be used for a very good cause.
- If you keep your shoes polished and well organized you'll find they will last much longer. Use a shoe rack for all your shoes or a shoe box to prevent them from getting dusty.
- Keep your belts on hooks and not on a belt ring. This causes clutter and makes it very difficult to get to a particular belt in a hurry. Do not roll up your belts into a ball as this will ruin them, especially leather belts because they will eventually crack.
- Fold scarves and place them flat, not over hangers where they will just slide off.

## UPDATE WHAT YOU HAVE

One of my favourite articles of clothing is a black jacket I purchased many years ago. The jacket had the most awful plastic buttons when I bought it but each season I update it with beautiful buttons, braiding or simply by adding or removing the collar. Look how different it looks!

*A basic black jacket.*

*The same jacket – the collar has been removed and the buttons have been changed.*

*The same jacket – this time with added collar and cuffs and different buttons.*

## THE LONG-TERM PLAN — WHERE TO START

You don't need a lot but what you have must work. In the table opposite, I have selected a total of 38 garments (you can have more if you wish) as a good base for either summer or winter wardrobe planning. If each item co-ordinates with three other items you have 114 outfits. If each item only co-ordinates with one other item you will still have 76 outfits.

It may take you a month, six months or perhaps even six years to achieve your long-term plan but be patient and do it step by step.

Start with the some of the basics like a navy blazer, white cotton shirt, black shift dress and a good pair of jeans, then build up the interest with a red coat, emerald green silk shirt, checked Chanel suit or printed body suit.

You may look at the first section, see 'Jackets' and despair because you don't wear them. Here, 'Jackets' includes a parka, casual wind breaker, a denim or leather jacket.

## SHOPPING AS AN INVESTMENT

The answer to the question of 'What am I going to wear today?' is simple. You need to know what the most important rules are when shopping.

- Shop wisely and economically. Each item you buy must go with three other garments in your wardrobe.
- Be confident. By now you should know whether the item you want to buy is right or wrong for you. Take your 'Wardrobe Planning Capsule' with you while shopping. Eventually you will become such a professional shopper you won't need it anymore.

---

**The 'Cost per Wear' principle**

Everyone has a fashion disaster or two lurking in their cupboard – something they splashed out on in a moment of recklessness and then never wore. But common sense teamed with simple arithmetic can save you money and make your wardrobe work for you. The 'Cost per Wear' principle is possibly the single most valuable lesson a fashion consumer can learn. Quite simply, it means dividing the cost of a garment by the number of times you are likely to wear it.

In other words, an expensive suit that can be worn in so many different ways, for example with its matching pencil skirt and also with a pair of jeans and a white casual shirt, becomes less costly than a closet full of bargains and must-haves that don't co-ordinate with anything else.

---

- Remember 'quality' not 'quantity'. Invest in classic designs and the best quality you can afford. If you buy an inferior quality garment, it may not even last a year, or once you have washed it four or five times, you may not be able to wear it again. Sometimes 'cheap' can be a waste of money.
- Remember the 'Cost per wear' principle! (See above)
- Buy fewer items and don't duplicate.
- Buy more tops than bottoms.
- Always buy styles that you feel comfortable wearing. If you are a sporty person and love jeans, leather jackets, oversized jumpers, and unstructured suits, then don't buy garments that you will never wear, such as formal outfits.
- Shop with an eraser in your mind. If you only like the top half and not the bottom half, leave the bottom half behind.
- To make trying on clothes easier, wear comfortable clothes that slip on and off easily.
- When trying on a garment, make sure that it fits you properly. I cannot stress the importance of this enough. Walk around, sit down, pretend you are driving your car.

A friend of mine had a velvet shift dress made. She has the most incredible body and wanted the dress to fit her like a glove. The dress was tapered and shaped and altered to perfection on her. She got dressed and got into her car only to find that she couldn't lift her hands up to the steering wheel – the sleeves were too tight! It was too late to change into another outfit as she was already running late so she had had to call a taxi to take her to the theatre.

- Do not buy impulsively.
- 'Sale!' Most women love this word. You can go ahead and purchase the item providing it goes with three other items in your wardrobe that are right for you. Don't buy something on sale if it does not suit you as you will probably never wear it. This type of purchase is a complete waste of money and takes up badly needed space in your wardrobe.
- Do not become a slave to fashion. If a style for that particular season is not right for you, don't buy it. There is never only one particular style which is 'in'. You will always have others to choose from.

# THE LONG-TERM PLAN

| STYLE | QUANTITY | COLOURS | LIFESTYLE |
|---|---|---|---|
| 9 Jackets | 3 Basic colours | Classic navy blazer | Smart or smart-casual |
| | | Black Chanel jacket | Smart or smart-casual |
| | | Black leather jacket | Smart-casual or casual |
| | 3 Hot colours | Red jacket | Smart or smart-casual |
| | | Magenta parka | Casual or casual-smart |
| | | Checked jacket | Casual-smart or casual |
| | 3 Cold colours | Emerald green | Smart or Smart-casual |
| | | Midnight blue | Smart or Smart-casual |
| | | Turquoise wind breaker | Casual |
| 15 Tops | 9 Plain | 5 White shirts / blouses | Smart through to casual |
| | | 2 Hot colours | Smart through to casual |
| | | 2 Cold colours | Smart through to casual |
| | 6 Print | Different designs | Smart through to casual |
| 10 Bottoms | 8 Plain | 2 Skirts: pencil & soft | Smart or smart-casual |
| | | 2 Skirts: pencil & soft | Casual |
| | | 2 Pants: tailored | Smart or smart-casual |
| | | 2 Pants: shorts & jeans | Casual |
| | 2 Print | Different classic designs | Smart or smart-casual |
| 4 Dresses | 2 Plain | Basic | Smart or casual |
| | 2 Print | 1 Fun & 1 classic | Smart or casual |
| Shoes | 8 pairs | 2 Court shoes | Smart |
| | | 1 Sling-back / sandal | Smart-casual |
| | | 2 Flat shoes | Smart and casual |
| | | 1 Boot | Smart and casual |
| | | 2 Trainers – 1 walking | Casual |
| | | 1 gym | Casual |
| Belts | 4 | 2 Basic leather | Smart or casual |
| | | 2 Fun: Chanel & fashion | Smart or casual |
| Bags | 4 | 2 Basic leather | Smart |
| | | 1 Drawstring | Casual |
| | | 1 Evening | Smart |

## CREATE 60 OUTFITS FROM ONLY 20 ITEMS!

This mix and match guide shows you how to create 60 different outfits with only 20 garments. The outfits are suitable for any occasion – the movies, a cocktail party, a casual or smart restaurant, the office, a wedding or even taking the kids to school.

It is quite useful to look at this capsule when packing to go away – for business, leisure or both. By following these principles you will have enough to wear, even with a limited wardrobe.

  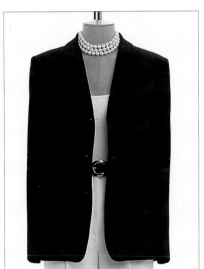

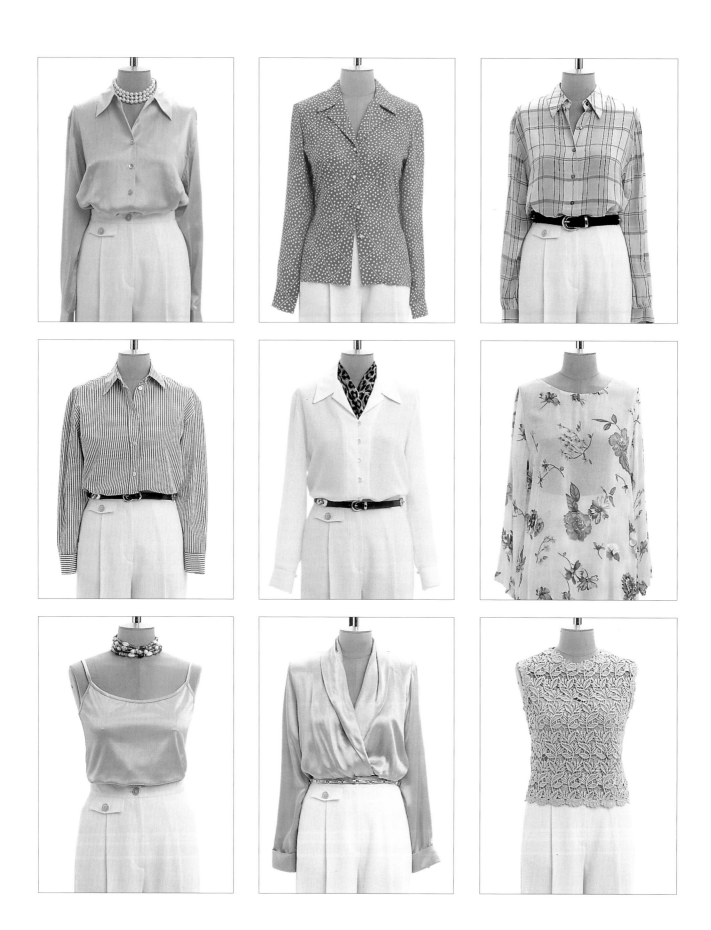

# PERSONAL MIX & MATCH CAPSULE

Use this blank example to create your own ideas (see pages 102–103).

1 JACKET

2 JACKET

3 JACKET

4 TOP

5 TOP

6 TOP

7 BOTTOM

8 BOTTOM

9 BOTTOM

10 BOTTOM

MIX & MATCH
COMBINATIONS

1 - 4 - 7
1 - 4 - 8
1 - 4 - 9
1 - 4 - 10
1 - 5 - 7
1 - 5 - 8
1 - 5 - 9
1 - 5 - 10
1 - 6 - 7
1 - 6 - 8
1 - 6 - 9
1 - 6 - 10
2 - 4 - 7
2 - 4 - 8
2 - 4 - 9
2 - 4 - 10
2 - 5 - 7
2 - 5 - 8
2 - 5 - 9
2 - 5 - 10
2 - 6 - 7
2 - 6 - 8
2 - 6 - 9
2 - 6 - 10
3 - 4 - 7
3 - 4 - 8
3 - 4 - 9
3 - 4 - 10
3 - 5 - 7
3 - 5 - 8
3 - 5 - 9
3 - 5 - 10
3 - 6 - 7
3 - 6 - 8
3 - 6 - 9
3 - 6 - 10

# CHAPTER SEVEN

# AM/PM DRESSING

*'Long after one has forgotten what a woman wore,*
*the memory of the image she created lingers'*
CHRISTIAN DIOR

HAVE YOU EVER been in a situation where you have had to go from work to an evening function and just haven't had the time to rush home and change? By making one or two subtle adjustments to your outfit, you can create the perfect look for that particular function.

If you want your look to be more formal, change what you are wearing on the top half of your body. Simply change your top and accessories and you will look completely different.

In the next few pages I have given some examples of different events you may attend and have chosen some basic outfits with which to work.

**FROM THE OFFICE TO THE THEATRE**

If you are wearing a pencil skirt, replace the jacket and blouse with a gold lace top. Put on some strappy shoes and in an instant your lifestyle has changed from smart to formal.

**FROM THE OFFICE TO A COCKTAIL PARTY**

If you are wearing your 'little black dress' (an essential item in any woman's wardrobe), all you need to do is add a jacket and other accessories to change from smart-casual to smart.

**FROM THE BOARDROOM TO A FORMAL FUNCTION**

Transform your look in an instant. Change the skirt to match your top and add different accessories. Dress up the outfit with black evening shoes and you are ready to go.

*Smart (office)*

*Smart (office)*

*Smart (office)*

*Smart (theatre)*

*Smart (cocktail)*

*Smart (formal function)*

## DRESSING DOWN FOR AN INFORMAL OCCASION

What do you do when the situation is reversed and you need to dress down for a more relaxed evening function? Simply change from a pencil skirt to tailored pants.

## FROM THE OFFICE TO A RESTAURANT

Remove your pencil skirt, pantyhose and high-heeled court shoes. Change into stone-coloured tailored pants with flat tan leather shoes and you have changed from smart to smart-casual.

## FROM THE OFFICE TO THE MOVIES

Replace the smart pants with jeans. Slip on a smart jacket and some comfortable flat leather shoes and you have the perfect look for a casual, relaxed evening with friends.

*Smart (office)*

*Smart (office)*

*Smart (office)*

*Smart-casual (informal function)*

*Smart-casual (restaurant)*

*Casual-smart (movies)*

# CHAPTER EIGHT

# PACKING

*'Never relinquish clothing to a valet without first specifically
saying you want it back!'*
FRAN LEBOWITZ

IN THIS CHAPTER I will share some
of my packing secrets with you and
show you how to pack for a:

♦ Two- to five-day trip;
♦ One- to three-week trip;
♦ Business trip for summer, winter or
a combined winter / summer trip;
♦ Business and leisure trip for
summer or winter, or a combined
winter / summer trip;
♦ Leisure trip only.

Travel is about efficiency and
lightweight luggage geared to speedy
air travel. Yet, despite how frequently
some people may travel, few seem to
manage the art of successful packing.

If you travel with only the essentials,
congratulations! If not, read on and
discover some handy tips to ensure
you never arrive with over-packed
baggage and crumpled clothes again.

From now on, when you arrive at
the airport everyone else will be
overloaded with luggage and will stare
with disbelief at your little bag.
However, you will be the only one
who looks different every day and
have no knots in your shoulders from
carrying excess baggage.

Pack according to percentages: for a
business trip pack 90% business and
10% leisure; for a combination trip
pack 50% business and 50% leisure;

and for a casual holiday 80% leisure
and 20% smart for eating out or going
to the theatre.

## PREPARING
## FOR YOUR TRIP

Here are some handy tips when
buying your luggage:

♦ Hand luggage: Look for a bag with
a strong, wide shoulder strap.
♦ Look for bags that are triple-
stitched, have a reinforced base,
tough, comfortable handles, and
good quality, chunky zips.

- Check that your bag has an outside pocket that is easily accessible.
- A dark colour won't show wear and tear so quickly.
- Fitted locks – these can make the difference between keeping your luggage and having it stolen. It is worth having a security lock fitted on your luggage – a lock where only one master key can be used.
- A suitcase with wheels and a built-in pulling handle alleviates the strain of carrying heavy luggage and can make even the most hectic journeys bearable.
- A collapsible, portable trolley can be very useful.

## TRAVEL LIGHT

There are three little words that get you into a lot of trouble when you pack – 'just in case'. You need to ask yourself three very important questions before each trip:

WHERE AM I GOING?
If you are going to the Caribbean on holiday it is unlikely that you will need to pack jerseys and heavy jackets. Shorts, T-shirts and other lightweight clothes are far more suitable.

HOW LONG WILL I BE AWAY?
Make a note of how many days you will be away, multiply it by three outfits a day (you will probably only use two) and total it. For example, if you are going away for two weeks (14 days) you need 42 outfits.

WHAT WILL MY LIFESTYLE BE ON THAT PARTICULAR TRIP?
You need to think about the lifestyle of each particular trip you take. If you are going on a business trip you are not going to need shorts and T-shirts.

If you are going on a leisure trip you need to take garments that will be suitable for a luncheon, a movie, a smart restaurant, or shopping in the market at a drop of a hat.

## HOW TO BEGIN

You need to lay out everything before you pack so that you can see what you are taking. Your clothes, your shoes, your accessories, everything! Make sure your bed or an area where you can lay out your garments is clear. Choose one of the packing checklists which follow and work through these handy tips. You now know how to co-ordinate and mix and match (see pages 98–103) so choosing outfits should be easy.

Begin with all your basic bottoms, then add the tops. If you want to take prints, work around the print first.

A FEW GOLDEN RULES:
- Make sure each item you take with you goes with three other items!
- First establish your basic foundation, then add the extras. Remember to have more tops than bottoms.
- First pack the clothing, then the accessories and shoes, and finally the extras (see pages 125–127).

## HOW TO PACK

- Pack the jackets first. Fold them inside out or in half (lengthways) to protect them. Pack into one half of the bag. Lay the next jacket on top, alternating the shoulder pads in order to save space. If you have a larger bag, pack flat.
- Follow the same procedure for your tops and bottoms by packing these in the other half of the bag.

- Leave jeans and trousers for last. Fold in half and lay across the length of the bag.
- Pack shoes, toe to heel, in a shoe bag (or plastic bag) and pack them into the four corners of the bag. You will have a corner left if you only pack three pairs of shoes. This doesn't mean you can pack an extra pair, this is where you should put your steam iron.
- Pack lingerie in the spaces between the shoes.
- Do not roll your belts or stuff them into your shoes, they will be ruined by the end of your trip. Wrap them around the inside of your bag.
- Pack your terry-towel gown last. Fold it in half as you would a towel.
- Cosmetics must always be packed in a separate vanity case to prevent leaked lotions or perfumes from damaging your clothes.

---

Tips

- All fabrics crease except for 100% polyester. Even if you pack your clothes flat, roll or fold them, they will always crease to some degree. A steamer is a worthwhile investment.
- Take blue or black jeans rather than coloured or printed jeans. Plains are far more versatile than prints or colours and make it easier to mix and match.
- Buy a leather travel bag which is designed to allow you to take it on the plane with you. This way you need not wait in the baggage area for your luggage.

---

**Please note:** Check with the particular airline you will travelling with as to what the maximum size and weight restrictions are for hand luggage.

I have used the following packing capsules for the last ten years and they have never let me down. Look under the relevant section and see exactly what to take and how much to take. Most importantly, it will all fit into a small bag, possibly far smaller than you have ever taken before.

> 'Tops' refers to jerseys, shirts and blouses.
> For a three-week trip – 24 garments
> co-ordinating with 3 other items = 72 outfits!

*This is a photograph of the bag on which my formula is based.*
*The dimensions are approximately 60 cm (24 in) long x*
*33 cm (13 in) wide x 26 cm (10¼ in) high.*

# Packing capsule: Business Trip

| Summer | Winter | Combination | Accessories |
|---|---|---|---|
| **2–5 Days** | **2–5 Days** | **2–5 Days** | **2–5 Days** |
| **3 Jackets:** Lightweight Lightweight Lightweight | **3 Jackets:** Coat Blazer Jacket | **3 Jackets:** Lightweight Jacket Coat | **3 Shoes:** Court: plain Court: interest Boots |
| **5 Tops:** 3 plain & 2 print | **5 Tops:** 3 plain & 2 print | **5 Tops:** 3 plain & 2 print | **4 Scarves:** Different designs |
| **3 Bottoms:** Pencil skirt Lightweight pants Jeans | **3 Bottoms:** Pencil skirt Warm pants Jeans | **3 Bottoms:** Pencil skirt Warm pants Jeans | **1 Bag:** Basic **2 Belts:** Smart & casual **Earrings** |
| **1–3 Weeks** | **1–3 Weeks** | **1–3 Weeks** | **1–3 Weeks** |
| *As above plus:* | *As above plus:* | *As above plus:* | *As above plus:* |
| 2 Jackets | 2 Jackets | 2 Jackets | Shoes: 1 pair |
| 7 Tops | 7 Tops | 7 Tops | |
| 3 Bottoms | 3 Bottoms | 3 Bottoms | Bag: 1 extra |
| 1 Dress | 1 Dress | 1 Dress | |
| **Extras:** 2 Bathing costumes Tracksuit 1 Sweatshirt Lingerie | 2 Jerseys Tracksuit 1 Sweatshirt Lingerie | 2 Bathing costumes 1 Jersey Tracksuit 1 Sweatshirt Lingerie | |

**Summary – Number of items: 24**

| | | | |
|---|---|---|---|
| Jackets: | 5 | Shoes: | 4 |
| Tops: | 12 | Scarves: | 4 |
| Bottoms: | 6 | Bags: | 2 |
| Dresses: | 1 | Belts: | 2 |
| Plus Extras | | | |

# Packing capsule: Business and Leisure trip

| Summer | Winter | Combination | Accessories |
|---|---|---|---|
| **2–5 Days** | **2–5 Days** | **2–5 Days** | **2–5 Days** |
| **3 Jackets:**<br>Lightweight<br>Lightweight<br>Lightweight | **3 Jackets:**<br>Coat<br>Cardigan<br>Jacket | **3 Jackets:**<br>Lightweight<br>Jacket<br>Coat | **3 Shoes:**<br>Court: Plain<br>Smart-casual flats<br>Boots |
| **5 Tops:**<br>3 plain & 2 print | **5 Tops:**<br>3 plain & 2 print | **5 Tops:**<br>3 plain & 2 print | **4 Scarves:**<br>Different designs |
| **3 Bottoms:**<br>Pencil skirt<br>Lightweight pants<br>Jeans | **3 Bottoms:**<br>Pencil skirt<br>Warm pants<br>Jeans | **3 Bottoms:**<br>Pencil skirt<br>Warm pants<br>Jeans | **1 Bag:** Everyday<br>**2 Belts:** Smart & casual<br><br>**Earrings** |
| **1–3 Weeks** | **1–3 Weeks** | **1–3 Weeks** | **1–3 Weeks** |
| *As above plus:* | *As above plus:* | *As above plus:* | *As above plus:* |
| 2 Jackets | 2 Jackets | 2 Jackets | Shoes: 1 pair |
| 7 Tops | 7 Tops | 7 Tops | |
| 3 Bottoms | 3 Bottoms | 3 Bottoms | Bag: 1 |
| 1 Dress | 1 Dress | 1 Dress | |
| **Extras:**<br>2 Bathing costumes<br>Tracksuit<br>1 Sweatshirt<br>Lingerie | 2 Jerseys<br>Tracksuit<br>1 Sweatshirt<br>Lingerie | 2 Bathing costumes<br>1 Jersey<br>Tracksuit<br>1 Sweatshirt<br>Lingerie | |

**Summary – Number of items: 24**

| | | | |
|---|---|---|---|
| Jackets: | 5 | Shoes: | 4 |
| Tops: | 12 | Scarves: | 4 |
| Bottoms: | 6 | Bags: | 2 |
| Dresses: | 1 | Belts: | 2 |
| Plus Extras | | | |

# Packing capsule: Leisure trip

| Summer | Winter | Combination | Accessories |
|---|---|---|---|
| **2–5 Days** | **2–5 Days** | **2–5 Days** | **2–5 Days** |
| **3 Jackets:**<br>Wind breaker<br>Lightweight<br>Cardigan | **3 Jackets:**<br>Coat<br>Blazer<br>Wind breaker | **3 Jackets:**<br>Lightweight<br>Coat<br>Blazer | **3 Shoes:**<br>Casual flats<br>Walking shoes<br>Boots |
| **5 Tops:**<br>3 plain & 2 print | **5 Tops:**<br>3 plain & 2 print | **5 Tops:**<br>3 plain & 2 print | **4 Scarves:**<br>Different designs |
| **3 Bottoms:**<br>Shorts<br>Lightweight pants<br>Jeans | **3 Bottoms:**<br>Warm skirt<br>Warm pants<br>Jeans | **3 Bottoms:**<br>Shorts<br>Warm pants<br>Jeans | **1 Bag:** Everyday<br>**2 Belts:** Smart & casual<br><br>**Earrings** |
| **1–3 Weeks** | **1–3 Weeks** | **1–3 Weeks** | **1–3 Weeks** |
| *As above plus:* | *As above plus:* | *As above plus:* | *As above plus:* |
| – | 2 Jackets | 2 Jackets | Shoes: 1 pair |
| 9 Tops | 7 Tops | 7 Tops | |
| 3 Bottoms | 3 Bottoms | 3 Bottoms | Bag: 1 beach |
| 1 Dress | 1 Dress | 1 Dress | |
| **Extras:**<br>2 Bathing costumes<br>Tracksuit<br>1 Sweatshirt<br>Lingerie | 2 Jerseys<br>Tracksuit<br>1 Sweatshirt<br>Lingerie | 2 Bathing costumes<br>1 Jersey<br>Tracksuit<br>1 Sweatshirt<br>Lingerie | |

**Summary – Number of items: 24**

**Summer**

| Jackets: | 3 | Shoes: | 4 |
|---|---|---|---|
| Tops: | 14 | Scarves: | 4 |
| Bottoms: | 6 | Bags: | 2 |
| Dresses: | 1 | Belts: | 2 |
| Plus Extras | | | |

**Winter and Combination**

| Jackets: | 5 | Shoes: | 4 |
|---|---|---|---|
| Tops: | 12 | Scarves: | 4 |
| Bottoms: | 6 | Bags: | 2 |
| Dresses: | 1 | Belts: | 2 |

# CHAPTER NINE

# BEAUTY & SKIN CARE

*'I needed a new look and I got one'*
MARIA CALLAS

## ESTABLISHING YOUR SKIN TYPE

### OILY SKIN

**Without make-up**
- Skin has an all-over oily shine.
- Skin has enlarged pores.
- Blackheads are visible.
- Tendency towards pimples on chin and forehead.
- Few or no fine lines.
- May have dry red patches from excessive use of astringents.
- Skin may have flakey areas caused by oily build-up.

**With make-up**
- Too much all-over shine.
- Make-up tends to look orange.
- Large pores are visible.
- Tendency to apply too much powder or make-up to mask oiliness and hide shine.
- Make-up seems to disappear from the centre of the face.
- Pebbly skin texture.

**Primary daily skin care needs:** Scrupulous cleansing; oil control and moisture maintenance.

# NORMAL / COMBINATION SKIN

**Without make-up**

- A very oily T-zone.
- Medium-sized pores.
- Some whiteheads and / or blackheads are visible.
- Isolated breakout of pimples.
- Very few lines.
- An all-over glow.
- Skin looks quite shiny in hot weather.
- Texture is neither fine nor very coarse.

**With make-up**

- A T-zone shine which is most intense on the nose.
- Enlarged pores on the nose are visible.
- Some whiteheads and / or blackheads are visible.
- A slight breakout of pimples on chin or forehead.
- A few lines, mostly concentrated in the eye area.
- An even, all-over glow.
- Hot weather intensifies shininess and causes make-up to disappear from the centre of the face.
- Quite good texture.

> **Primary daily skin care needs:** Thorough cleansing; balanced toning and moisturising; light emollient replenishment.

# DRY SKIN

**Without make-up**

- Fine, even texture.
- Small pores.
- A slight roughness or chapping in the cheek area.
- Some lines around the eyes.
- An overall matte look with a slight T-zone in hot weather.
- A throat which may be starting to line.

**With make-up**

- Very little or no glow.
- Small pores.
- Fine lines around the eyes.
- A tendency for make-up to collect in expression lines.
- Throat tends to look older than the face.
- Skin becomes chapped and dry very quickly when exposed to wind and cold weather.

> **Primary daily skin care needs:** Gentle cleansing and toning; emollient rich moisturing.

# EXTRA DRY SKIN

**Without make-up**

- Very fine textured skin.
- Pores that are almost invisible.
- A dry, almost translucent quality.
- Many fine lines and possibly deep expression lines.
- Roughness or flaking due to obvious dryness.
- A leathery look.
- Possible capillary breakages, particularly around the nose.
- A lined throat.

**With make-up**

- A very dry, almost powdery look.
- A fine textured, translucent quality.
- Invisible pores.
- Make-up collects and cakes in lines or wrinkles.
- Uneven cheek colour due to roughness.
- Many fine lines, particularly around the eyes.
- A lined or wrinkled throat.
- Broken capillaries around the nose.

> **Primary daily skin care needs:** Extremely gentle cleansing and toning; very rich moisture care at all times.

# THE ESSENTIALS EVERY WOMAN NEEDS

### FACIAL WASHES
Remove dirt, grime and stale make-up from the skin's surface.

### CREAM CLEANSERS
Ideal for dry complexions. Leaves the skin purified, detoxified and thoroughly cleansed.

### TONERS AND ASTRINGENTS
Refresh and cool your skin. They rinse off all traces of cleanser and restore the skin's acid mantle. Toners stimulate circulation and refine skin texture.

### MOISTURISERS
Form a barrier film on the surface of your skin to prevent moisture loss. They leave the skin soft and smooth.

### FACE MASKS
These deep cleanse or nourish your skin. They leave the skin re-energised with vitality, tone and elasticity.

### FACIAL SCRUBS AND EXFOLIATORS
These dislodge dead surface skin cells and reveal the younger, fresher cells underneath.

### EYE MAKE-UP REMOVERS
Removes stubborn eye make-up while maintaining the delicate balance of skin around the eyes.

### EYE CREAMS
These gels and creams contain special ingredients to plump out fine lines and keep the skin soft. They also reduce puffiness and shadows under the eye.

### NIGHT CREAMS
These are designed to give your skin extra pampering while you sleep.

*Revlon Absolutes: for absolutely beautiful skin.*

## SOFT PERSON – COOL SKIN TONE

You should opt for baby pastel tones or soft, neutral tones. Use sheer formulations if your skin tone is clear and translucent. This way you will flatter your colouring with a light, fresh make-up look, without overpowering it.

**Before:** *Cool skin tone*

| | |
|---|---|
| *Foundation:* | Soft peach undertone |
| *Face powder:* | Translucent |
| *Blusher:* | Cool pink, cream |
| *Eye make-up:* | Soft blue, ivory, soft brown, grey tones |
| *Mascara:* | Brown, black |
| *Lip liner:* | Pink-brown |
| *Lipstick:* | Cool pink, red, cherry |

**After:** *Cool skin tone*

**Eyes  Lips**

# MAKE-UP ADVICE

## SOFT PERSON – WARM SKIN TONE

If you have a warmer tone to your skin, you should opt for tawny, neutral shades which will enhance your basic colouring.

**Before:** *Warm skin tone*

| | |
|---|---|
| *Foundation:* | Soft pink undertone |
| *Face powder:* | Translucent |
| *Blusher:* | Pink-brown |
| *Eye make-up:* | Peach, soft brown, gold and beige tones |
| *Mascara:* | Brown, black |
| *Lip liner:* | Nude, neutral shades |
| *Lipstick:* | Rose, bronze, peach, light nude shades |

**After:** *Warm skin tone*

Eyes     Lips

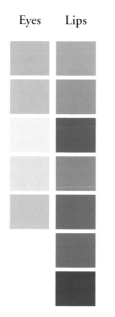

# MAKE-UP ADVICE

MEDIUM PERSON – COOL SKIN TONE
You will look fabulous with strong shades of cosmetics, the density of colour providing a striking contrast to your skin tone.

**Before:** *Cool skin tone*

*Foundation:* Neutral shade with a slight blue undertone

*Face powder:* Translucent

*Blusher:* Pink-plum shade

*Eye make-up:* Cool ivory, a touch of taupe or charcoal

*Mascara:* Black, charcoal

*Lip liner:* Plum or berry shades

*Lipstick:* Cherry, mauve, wine, blackberry, rose

**After:** *Cool skin tone*

### Eyes   Lips

# MAKE-UP ADVICE

MEDIUM PERSON – WARM SKIN TONE

Your skin tone will look beautiful with burnished browns, warm reds and earthy shades.

**Before:** *Warm skin tone*

| | |
|---|---|
| *Foundation:* | Tawny shade with a yellow undertone |
| *Face powder:* | Warm |
| *Blusher:* | Warm, tawny brown |
| *Eye make-up:* | Red-brown, coppers |
| *Mascara:* | Black, brown |
| *Lip liner:* | Red or brown shades |
| *Lipstick:* | Fiery red, red-brown, sienna, rose, hot pink, amber, coffee |

**After:** *Warm skin tone*

**Eyes    Lips**

# MAKE-UP ADVICE

## DEEP PERSON – COOL SKIN TONE

Your natural golden tan or deeper, darker skin will look fantastic with rich, warm shades and tones. Redheads with a cool skin tone can experiment with brighter colours to contrast with their wonderful colouring.

**Before:** *Cool skin tone*

| | |
|---|---|
| *Foundation:* | Ivory, cool shades |
| *Face powder:* | Translucent, ivory |
| *Blusher:* | Peachy shade |
| *Eye make-up:* | Neutral, peach tones, hint of gold |
| *Mascara:* | Brown |
| *Lip liner:* | Orange-brown, orange-red |
| *Lipstick:* | Burnished orange, coral, sienna, red, ruby |

**After:** *Cool skin tone*

Eyes    Lips

# MAKE-UP ADVICE

DEEP PERSON – WARM SKIN TONE

Your vibrant colouring is suited to bold shades of wine, purple and brown. These blue-toned colours will look fabulous with your skin and hair tones.

**Before:** *Warm skin tone*

| | |
|---|---|
| *Foundation:* | Beige, warm shades |
| *Face powder:* | Warm |
| *Blusher:* | Brown-toned blusher, bronzing powder |
| *Eye make-up:* | Wine, pale mauve |
| *Mascara:* | Brown |
| *Lip liner:* | Plum shades |
| *Lipstick:* | Deep plum, burgundy, wine shades |

**After:** *Warm skin tone*

Eyes   Lips

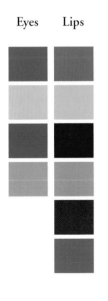

# MAKE-UP ADVICE

### DEEP PERSON – OLIVE SKIN, DARK HAIR
Your skin tone is suited to rich browns, oranges and a hint of gold or bronze that will define your features beautifully.

**Before:** *Olive skin*

| | |
|---|---|
| *Foundation:* | Gold and honey shades |
| *Face powder:* | Gold, warm |
| *Blusher:* | Peach-brown |
| *Eye make-up:* | Golden shades, warm brown, dark bronze |
| *Mascara:* | Black |
| *Lip liner:* | Brown, sienna |
| *Lipstick:* | Sunny orange, bronzes and coppers |

**After:** *Olive skin*

Eyes    Lips

# MAKE-UP ADVICE

DEEP PERSON – PALE BLACK SKIN, BLACK HAIR
Emphasize your looks with earthy shades. Your gold or red toned skin works wonderfully with beige, brown or copper colours.

| | |
|---|---|
| *Foundation:* | Caramel |
| *Face powder:* | Caramel |
| *Blusher:* | Pink-brown |
| *Eye make-up:* | Ivory-tones mixed with deep brown |
| *Mascara:* | Black |
| *Lip liner:* | Pink-brown |
| *Lipstick:* | Neutral pink-brown |

**Before:** *Pale black skin*

**After:** *Pale black skin*

Eyes    Lips

# MAKE-UP ADVICE

DEEP PERSON – DEEP BLACK SKIN, BLACK HAIR

Experiment with colour possibilities as your dark skin, eyes and hair provide the perfect canvas on which to work. Choose bold, deep colours to achieve a wonderful glow.

**Before:** *Deep black skin*

| | |
|---|---|
| *Foundation:* | Mahogany |
| *Face powder:* | Dark |
| *Blusher:* | Tawny brown |
| *Eye make-up:* | Dark blackcurrant, accent of golden shades |
| *Mascara:* | Black |
| *Lip liner:* | Plum |
| *Lipstick:* | Dark plum, wine, berry |

**After:** *Deep black skin*

Eyes    Lips

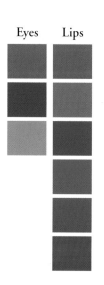

## YOUR BEAUTY QUESTIONS ANSWERED

Q How much make-up is enough?

A Do not over-emphasize your features for an everyday look. You can, however, wear more make-up at night.

Combinations to enhance your assets:

◆ Light eyes, light mouth: Apply a little colour to your cheeks otherwise you will look drained.
◆ Light eyes, darker mouth: A natural-looking face with extra emphasis on the lips.
◆ Dark eyes, light mouth: This is a sophisticated look but it is better suited to younger women. Older women need to apply lip colour.
◆ Dark eyes, dark mouth: only emphasize one asset – your face needs a focus feature.

Q I often use too much blusher. How can I remove the excess without washing my whole face?

A Rub gently over the blusher to remove colour and soften it further by applying translucent powder.

Q How do I apply blusher properly?

A It all depends on the shape of your face.

◆ Round face: Blend blusher upwards from your cheeks into your hairline.
◆ Square face: Concentrate your blusher in a circle on the rounded parts of your cheeks.
◆ Sweetheart face: Dust your blusher slightly lower than your cheek bones and into the hollows of your cheeks.

◆ Oval face: Apply blusher to the most prominent part of your cheekbone, blending upwards towards the temple.

Q How can I make my lipstick last all day?

A Try the new generation lip colours which last all day long – Revlon's Colorstay is a good choice.

Q I made the mistake of plucking too much hair from my eyebrows. What can I do to fix it?

A Choose a natural-looking brown brow pencil and apply it lightly across the brow. Brows should always be well groomed. Have your brows shaped by a professional the first time around to get the right arch, and then maintain them at home by plucking any stragglers that fall below the curve.

◆ Round face: Aim the end of the brow towards the tip of your ear.
◆ Oval face: The brow should curve down towards the lower ear.
◆ Square face: Slope the brow towards the middle of the ear.
◆ Sweetheart face: Shape the brow in a straight line towards the top of the ear.

Q Are there make-up colours some people should never wear?

A As a general rule, everyone can wear every colour, but it depends on the shade and intensity. For instance, everyone can wear red lipstick but the shade will vary according to your skin tone. A soft, pink-red will suit a pale-skinned blonde, whereas a warm-toned redhead will be able to carry off an orange based, fiery shade.

Q My lips are always dry and lipstick generally looks awful. Is there a solution to this problem?

A Exfoliate your lips very gently, removing any hard flakes of skin. You can also try Revlon's Moondrops lipstick which contains Vitamin E and Aloe to treat dry lips.

## BEAUTY TIPS

◆ Dust blusher over your eyelids as an instant subtle eye shadow.
◆ If you want to experiment with new make-up, ask the consultant at the beauty counter for advice. It is the best way to see how colours and formulations look on your skin.
◆ Remove all make-up under your eyes for a younger look.
◆ Mix different colour lipsticks to create new shades.
◆ Try Revlon's range of Intense Therapy nail treatments for hard-to-grow nails.
◆ Lip and eye pencils are less likely to break if you put them in the refrigerator before sharpening.
◆ If you have very soft nails, file them while the polish is still on to prevent them cracking. Never file wet nails.
◆ If you find eyebrow tweezing painful, numb the area with an ice cube before you begin.
◆ Warm up your looks by dusting a little blusher over your temples, chin and the tip of your nose, as well as your cheeks.
◆ If you look tired, blend in a little concealer just away from the outer corner of your eye – it will look as though you had a good night's sleep.
◆ Do not apply make-up before blow-drying your hair. The heat from the dryer can make you perspire and cause your make-up to smudge.

- Allow your moisturiser to sink in to your skin before applying your make-up – it will help your make-up go on more easily.
- To prevent lipstick getting on your teeth, put your finger in your mouth, purse your lips and then pull it out.
- You can dry nail enamel quickly by blasting your nails with a jet of cold air from your hairdryer. Otherwise, try Revlon's Topspeed nail enamel and Topspeed Topcoat for 90-second drying time.
- Remove excess mascara by placing a tissue between your upper and lower lashes and then blinking two or three times.
- Prevent your lipstick from 'melting' by dusting lips with a little loose powder. This will give it a drier texture and help it stay on longer.
- If you find obvious edges to the foundation on your chin, jaw line or hairline, blend them away with a damp cosmetic sponge.

## APPLYING BLUSHER

### OVAL FACE
**Do**
- Apply blusher directly to cheekbones and blend out from there. It should never end closer to the nose than two finger-widths and should not reach lower than the tip.
- Blend in your blusher thoroughly by brushing away any definite demarcation lines.

**Don't**
- Apply blusher too high on your cheeks. Leave this area lighter to highlight your eyes.
- Overdo the blusher as the colour will be too strong. Mute it with a dusting of face powder.

*Oval face*

### SWEETHEART FACE
**Do**
- Apply blusher straight over the cheekbones to balance the face.
- Soften a pointy chin with a hint of blusher.
- Tone down a bright blusher with a dusting of face powder.

**Don't**
- Forget to blend carefully and erase any harsh lines.

*Sweetheart face*

### ROUND FACE
**Do**
- Apply blusher by sweeping from the centre of the cheekbone and up and out to the temples.

*Round face*

**Don't**
- Let the blusher level sink below the tip of the nose.
- Use too much blusher as it will close in a round face.

*Square face*

### SQUARE FACE
**Do**
- Brush an inverted arc from the middle of the cheekbone to the hairline to soften and lengthen the face.
- Apply blusher to the cheekbones and sweep it horizontally toward the hairline to create a wider look.
- Apply a hint of blusher to the chin and forehead to 'shorten' the face.

**Don't**
- Let the blusher reach higher than eye level.

# EYES

## BALANCED EYES

### Do

- Start any eye make-up on a 'clean canvas' – a neutral shadow base from lashes to brows may be enough. Or you may want to smooth over any lines or shadows with concealer.
- Use at least two shades of eye shadow; a medium shade on the entire eyelid and a darker shade in the crease and on the outer third of the lid will create depth.
- Place the mascara wand close to the base of the lashes and wiggle it through to colour and separate them.
- Apply darker and thicker liner for evenings.
- Brighten up an evening eye with highlighter applied under the eyebrow's arch.

*Balanced eyes*

### Don't

- Draw a hard lid line. Apply a thin smudge of liner all around the eye, keeping close to the lashes.

## DEEP-SET EYES

### Do

- Pay attention to the shape and appearance of your eyebrows. Shape and soften the brows with a brown eyebrow pencil.
- Make sure that brows point out, never down. Classic brows start at a point just above the inner corner of the eye and end slightly beyond the outer corner.
- Use light colours on your lids and a highlighter just under the brow.
- Use medium or dark colours in the eye crease.
- Apply a gold eye shadow over the lid and a rusty shade along the socket.
- Bring lids 'forward' with a light shadow shade and push back the prominent bone with darker shadow applied just above the crease.

- Smudge liner for a softer, more natural look. Line the lash lines with a reddish-brown shadow, smudged for a softened effect.
- Coat top lashes only, using black mascara.

*Deep-set eyes*

### Don't

- Use shimmering, pearly eye shadows.
- Use a dark shadow in the crease as your deep eye crease creates its own shadow.
- Use liner on the inner third of the eye. To create an almond shape apply liner in a thin-to-thick line on the outer two-thirds of the eye.
- Skimp on mascara. Two or three coats is essential.

## SMALL EYES

### Do

- Shape brows with a brown eyebrow pencil and apply a pale pink shadow to the eye crease, blending it up and outward over the eyebrow arches.
- Use two neutral shades. Apply the paler one as a base and brush the darker one across the top of your eyelids and into the crease of the lid to open up the eyes.
- To make your eyes stand out, highlight the area under your brow with a frosted shade or highlighter.
- Bring out the best in your eyes with an all-over lid sweep of light-toned shadow.
- Keep the inner corners light, and add a little contouring with darker shadow on outer third of the lid and crease. Blend upwards and outwards.

*Small eyes*

- Use only medium colours in the eye crease.
- Apply brown eye shadow to the outer corners of the eyes and smudge some along the bottom lash line.
- Sweep black mascara through both the top and bottom eyelashes.

### Don't
- Let your eyebrows overshadow your eyes. Tweeze any stray hairs and trim any long brow hairs if necessary (brush hairs upwards and snip ends carefully).
- Apply dark colours to the eye crease.
- Use dark shades on the lids as this will make the eye appear smaller. Rather use colours that are matte and light.
- Close in the eye with a rim of eye liner all around the eye. Apply liner to the top and bottom of the outer third only.
- Skimp on mascara. Keep it heavy on the top lashes and light on the lower lashes.

### CLOSE SET EYES
**Do**
- Apply a light colour over the entire lash-to-brow area.
- Apply paler shades from the inner corner of the eye to the mid-eye area and increase colour intensity as you blend up and around. Keep darker shades away from the inner corner of the eye.
- Apply eyeliner from mid-lid and extend the line to slightly past the end of the eye. Thicken the width of the liner as it reaches the outer corner of the eye.

### Don't
- Let your eyebrows draw your eyes closer together. Tweeze stray eyebrow hairs from the inner ends to widen the space between them.
- Apply liner to the inner half of the eye as it will bring your eyes closer together.
- Apply mascara on the inner lashes; reserve it for the outer two-thirds only.

### WIDE SET EYES
**Do**
- Use a brow pencil to bring wide set eyebrows closer together.
- Start any eye make-up with a lash-to-brow wash of light shadow base.
- Apply darker shadow at the inner corner of the eye and blend it lightly across the lids.
- Concentrate liner on the inner half of the lid.

*Wide set eyes*

### Don't
- Apply too much make-up to the outer corners of the eyes as this will emphasize the space between them.
- Shy away from the colourful new shades of eye make-up. Some are real eye-openers.
- Blend eye shadow until all the colour is in place. Too much blending pushes colour around and creates a muddy appearance.
- Use only one coat of mascara.

### VANISHING LIDS
**Do**
- Experiment with different optical illusions to curve the lid shape and create depth. Start with a mid-toned shadow, applied lid to brow. Then arc a deeper, neutral shadow just under the brow bone from the bridge of the nose to the end of the eye. Highlight under the eyebrow and draw a thin line of black near the lashes.
- Smudge and blend the colours to create a softer, more natural look.
- Curl lashes with an eyelash curler and apply copious amounts of lash-lengthening mascara.

*Vanishing lids*

### Don't
- Dismiss the simple definition created by a smudged band of softened black or deep natural eye liner.

## NOSE

### BROAD NOSE

- Use a second shade of foundation one shade darker that your natural skin tone. Sweep along the sides of the nose with a small, firm make-up brush, starting just below the inner corners of the eyebrows, and continue down to the edges of the nostrils.
- Dab a lighter shade of foundation down the centre of the nose, again blending well.

### NARROW NOSE

- To make the bridge appear wider, shade the centre of the nose with a concealer that's slightly darker than your natural skin tone. Then highlight the sides of your nose and nostrils with a lighter shade.

### BUMPY NOSE

- To make the bump appear less prominent, apply a concealer that is a few shades darker than your natural skin tone.

## LIPS

### UNEVEN LIPS
**Do**
- Apply concealer over the lip line and set with powder.
- Balance lips by drawing a line just outside the thinner lips and just inside the fuller lip. Brush on lipstick inside the lines.

**Don't**
- Go without lip liner.

### FULL LIPS
**Do**
- Cover the lips lightly with foundation to blur the edges. Use a lip liner to trace inside the lip line.

Brush on lipstick, being careful not to go outside the line. Set with powder.
- Use medium shades with a soft matte finish to make the lips appear slightly thinner.

**Don't**
- Let your lips become dry.

*Full Lips*

### THIN LIPS
**Do**
- Strengthen the appearance of your lips with mid-tone range colours.
- To create a pout, outline the top lip with liner to emphasize the 'm'.
- To make your lips appear fuller, outline just outside the natural edge of the lower lip. Brush on a strong lip colour for even more definition.
- Using glossy colours will give your lips a fuller, firmer look.

**Don't**
- Use a colour that's too dark as it will make your lips seem thinner.

*Thin lips*

### SMALL LIPS
**Do**
- Vary the layers of pencil and lipstick.
- Try broadening your smile by building out the sides of your natural lip line with lip pencil.

**Don't**
- Use shimmering colours as too much shine acts as an optical eraser. Look for soft matte finishes.

- Wear a lipstick that is too dark as dark colours will make your lips appear smaller.

*Small lips*

### DOWN-TURNED LIPS
**Do**
- Use a lip pencil to outline the subtle little up-turns at the extending corners of your mouth. Do this while you are smiling.
- Make sure the outline of your lower lip rises smoothly into the upturned corners.
- Focus attention on the centre of your lips by keeping the corners light and the centre dark.

**Don't**
- Forget to start all lip looks with a touch of foundation or concealer over your natural lip line. This will always keep the lipstick in place for longer.

*Down-turned lips*

### EVEN LIPS
**Do**
- Keep your lip line immaculate. Smudges can be camouflaged with a touch of foundation or concealer.
- Top off your lip pencil base with a little lipstick or gloss.

**Don't**
- Be afraid to outline your lips. It gives them more definition.

# CHAPTER TEN

# HAIR

*'A style reflects the image a woman has of herself'*
GLORIA VANDERBILT

ONE OF THE first questions women ask my hairdresser is, 'What should I do with my hair?'. It is interesting to note that most women are unhappy or bored with their natural shade or current hair style. If they have straight hair they wish it were curly, and if they are blonde they wish they were brunette. I believe it is important to constantly update your look and, to be honest, very little beats a good hair cut – you feel and look fantastic. First of all, you need to identify the hair colour that suits your natural skin tone and then you need to establish the hair style to best complement the shape of your face.

### CHOOSING THE CORRECT HAIR COLOUR TO SUIT YOUR SKIN TONE

**Pink skin**
*Yes:* Choose neutral tones – ash blonde, ash brown or dark brown.
*No:* Red or yellow-blonde are usually a total disaster.

**Olive skin**
*Yes:* Stay dark. A few rich, low lights in chestnut or burgundy can add interest, as long as the colour complements your skin tone.
*No:* Blonde or light shades will not suit you.

**Pale white, ivory or creamy skin**
This skin tone will go with any hair colour as your skin has no pink in it.

**Yellow and sallow skin**
*Yes:* Dark, rich shades such as burgundy or deep auburn.
*No:* Colours with a yellow undertone.

---

Tip

Make-up, eyebrow and hair colour should complement one another.

---

*If your natural colour is black you can change to: glossy black or blue-black.*

*If your natural colour is dark to light blonde you can change to: wheat, light golden blonde, ash blonde, pale blonde, honey or light golden brown.*

*If your natural colour is blonde to grey you can change to: light golden blonde, ash blonde, light golden brown, brown/beige or copper.*

CLAIROL

*If your natural colour is light brown you can change to: light golden brown, honey, medium golden brown, auburn or black.*

*If your natural colour is dark brown you can change to: medium golden brown, auburn, dark honey, chocolate brown, reddish brown or black.*

*If your natural colour is red you can change to: hazelnut, chestnut, auburn, mahogany or reddish brown/dark brown.*

CLAIROL

# Hair styles to suit your face shape

## OVAL FACE

This is the most versatile face shape as almost any hair style will suit you – short, medium or long.

Before

After

After

Before

## What you should do

◆ Have height over the top of your head. This will make your face appear longer and slimmer.

◆ Side partings will make your cheekbones look narrower.

◆ Wear styles that are long and soft into the neck.

◆ Pull some tendrils onto your forehead to soften the width.

◆ A soft side fringe across your forehead will detract attention from your small chin and prevent a hard, symmetrical look.

◆ Flip your hair out at the jawline if you have a bob – the extra volume gives the illusion of a wider jawline.

## What you shouldn't do

◆ If your hair is flat over the top of your head your face will look shorter and fuller.

◆ Very short hair or a middle parting will accentuate your pointy chin.

◆ A short, solid fringe will make your cheeks appear fuller.

After

Before

## What you should do

- Have length into your neck – your face will look more oval.
- Feather hair around your cheekbones to create the illusion of slimness.
- Height over your head will give volume to your crown and will make your cheeks appear slimmer.
- Wear an asymmetrical style. Tuck your hair behind one ear and let the rest fall over your forehead to the opposite side. Your cheekbones will be more defined.

## What you shouldn't do

- Short (men's short) styles will make your face look rounder.
- A flat style will make your face appear shorter and fuller.
- A curly, round style will not give your cheeks any definition.
- Middle partings add to the breadth of the face.

After

Before

After

### What you should do

◆ Longer, layered hair will soften
an otherwise quite severe
bone structure.

◆ Add height to your crown with
side partings. This will appear to
lengthen your face, making it look
longer and slimmer.

### What you shouldn't do

◆ A short back and sides style is
too masculine.

◆ A flat style, full fringe or middle
parting will create extra width
and squareness.

◆ An open neck will make your
jawline look even stronger.

# BE CREATIVE WITH YOUR HAIRSTYLE

Casual to smart in an instant!

Before

After

After

Before

After

After

Colouring
your hair
is as easy as
1...2...3

CLAIROL

Before

After

After

Before

After

After

Before

After

After

# INDEX